Quick & easy

KIDS' CAKES

Sara Lewis

Quick & easy

KIDS' CAKES

50 great cakes for children of all ages

hamlyn

First published in Great Britain in 2006 by Hamlyn, a division of
Octopus Publishing Group Ltd, 2–4 Heron Quays, London E14 4JP

Distributed in the United States and Canada by Sterling Publishing Co.,
Inc., 387 Park Avenue South, New York, NY 10016-8810

ISBN-13: 978-0-600-61564-4
ISBN-10: 0-600-61564-2

A CIP catalogue record for this book is available from the British Library

Printed and bound in China

10 9 8 7 6 5 4 3 2 1

Dedication

For Nicky and her powers of persuasion.

Notes

Standard level spoon and cup measurements are used in all recipes.

Medium eggs should be used unless otherwise stated.

Ovens should be preheated to the specified temperature—if using a
fan-assisted oven, follow the manufacturer's instructions for adjusting
the time and the temperature.

Contents

Introduction

For young children or the young at heart, nothing beats the thrill of blowing out the candles on your birthday cake, but as a busy working parent, the idea of finding the time to make a cake that is extra special can fill you with horror.

Over the next few pages, you will find 50 quick and easy cakes to delight tiny tots and melt the heart of even the coolest older child. Some can be decorated in 20 minutes or so, while others will take around an hour. The cakes may be baked and frozen in advance to spread the workload, and most can be made with equipment that you will already have in your kitchen cabinets. Alternatively, cheat and buy a plain cake from your local supermarket. All cakes can be made by even the most inexperienced of cake makers—you may just find that it takes you a few minutes longer to do. Don't be put off if you have never made a cake before. If you can roll out frozen pastry, you can roll out and cover a cake with ready-to-use icing. Very often it is the simplest cake that is the most eye-catching.

In the first section of the book, you will find all the basic recipes for making the cakes themselves, with tips on flavor variations, recipes for different frostings and fillings, plus advice and techniques on achieving that special finish. The main section features cake designs for both younger and older children, boys and girls, decorated with butter frosting, ready-to-use icing, chocolate, and candies. There is something for everyone, from a cute pastel-colored tortoise to an inviting white chocolate puppy; from jeweled pink crowns or mini birthday cakes to a candy-guzzling monster, a grown-up game of chess, and a scary ghostly face.

But you don't have to wait for a birthday to try these cakes. They make great school raffle prizes or can simply be made with the children as a fun way to cheer up a dreary day in the school vacation. Whatever the occasion, making and decorating your own cake is a great way to show just how much you care.

Equipment

The recipes in this book are generally quick and easy to make and assemble, so the amount of equipment you will need is minimal. You will probably find that you already have most of the items of equipment you need, with perhaps the exception of some of the specialty tiny icing cutters. If you are new to cake making, it is worth checking which pans are required before you begin baking so that you are not disappointed.

If there is a piece of equipment you need to buy, it's well worth visiting your local cake-decorating store. They are usually packed with cutters, tools, ready-made decorations, colored icings, and almost every shade of food coloring imaginable. However, if you don't have a convenient local store, you will find that many of the larger kitchenware companies offer a comprehensive mail-order service.

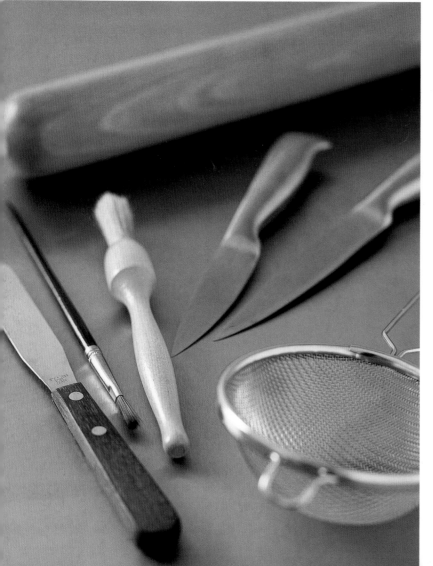

BASIC EQUIPMENT

- kitchen scale
- baking pans
- waxed paper and nonstick parchment paper
- paper bake cups
- scissors
- pastry brush
- artists' paintbrushes
- selection of bowls in various sizes
- large and small strainer—a new tea strainer is ideal
- large serrated knife for cutting cakes in half, dull knife for spreading butter frosting, large and small cook's knives for cutting icing shapes
- large and small spatulas
- large and small rolling pins
- whisk
- cookie cutters and selection of small/mini cutters

Tip

If you like cooking, the chances are that you will already have most of the equipment that you need, with the exception of specialty cutters or cake boards.

CAKE PANS

Most cake pans can be found in the
cookware department of your local
large department store or hardware store
or large supermarket. For more unusual
equipment, visit a specialty cookware
or cake-decorating store, or check out
appropriate websites on the Internet. If
buying new pans, opt for the better-quality
ranges, as they will last for 20 years or
more without denting or warping. A
removable-bottomed pan makes it easier
to remove a cake, but is not essential.
Likewise, flexible muffin and cupcake
molds are easy to use, but rigid metal
ones work just as well.

MOST FREQUENTLY USED CAKE PANS

- 9 inch deep round pan
- 8 inch deep square pan
- 2 x 8 inch straight-sided
  layer pans
- 7 inch deep round pan
- 12-section muffin pan
- 12 x 9 x 2 inch roasting pan

Lining a deep round pan

Brush the sides and base of the pan lightly with a little oil, then cut strips of waxed paper a little taller than the side of the pan. Fold a strip about ½ inch in from one long edge, then snip up to the fold line at intervals. Stand the paper in the pan so that the cut edges sit flat on the base of the pan. Cut and add extra paper strips, overlapping the ends of the strips slightly, as necessary to cover the entire side of the pan. Using the pan as a guide, stand it on some more waxed paper, draw around the pan, then cut out the round and press onto the base of the pan. Brush the paper lightly with more oil. If using nonstick parchment paper instead of waxed paper, simply add the paper shapes to the dry pan.

Lining a deep square pan

Cut strips of paper a little taller than the sides of the pan, just as when lining a round pan, but snip up to the fold line only where the paper is pressed into the corners of the pan. Cut a square of paper for the base in just the same way as for a round pan.

Lining a roasting pan

Cut a piece of nonstick parchment paper a little larger than the pan, then make diagonal cuts into the corners. Press the paper into the pan, tucking the snipped edges one behind the other so that the base and sides of the pan are completely lined in one action. You can use waxed paper instead of nonstick parchment paper, but you will need to grease both the pan and the paper.

Lining a layer pan

Brush the base and side of the pan with a little oil, then stand the pan on top of a piece of waxed paper, draw around the pan and cut out the round of paper. Lay over the base of the pan and brush lightly with a little extra oil.

Cake recipes

Most of the cakes in this book are based on two simple cake mixes: a Madeira cake and a quick-mix layer cake. These mixtures are then baked in a variety of different items of bakeware—you'll be surprised to find just how many shapes can be conjured up from a few cake pans, pudding basins, the odd mixing bowl, and a roasting pan. Make and bake the cake the day before the party or freeze it a week or so in advance, un-iced. This section also includes recipes for individual cakes—cupcakes and muffins—plus a jelly roll. For people short of time, store-bought equivalents have been listed, where available, on main recipes.

MADEIRA CAKES

This traditional creamed cake is made by beating butter or soft margarine with sugar until light and fluffy. Gradually mix in beaten eggs and self-rising flour until smooth. Alternating eggs and flour will prevent the eggs curdling or separating the mixture. Unlike a single-stage cake, this has a greater proportion of flour to fat and sugar and produces a light, slightly closer-textured cake that can be cut and shaped well, making it ideal for that special birthday cake.

Small Madeira Cake

¾ cup soft margarine or butter, at room temperature

¾ cup superfine sugar

3 eggs

1 tablespoon milk

2 cups self-rising flour

FLAVORINGS

Vanilla **1 teaspoon vanilla extract**

Lemon **grated zest of ¾ lemon; replace milk with 1 tablespoon lemon juice**

Orange **grated zest of ¾ orange; replace milk with 1 tablespoon orange juice**

Chocolate **replace ½ cup flour with same quantity of cocoa powder**

The above amount will fill:

SIZE OF CONTAINER	BAKING TIME
7 inch deep round cake pan	45–50 minutes
6 inch deep square cake pan	45–50 minutes
8 inch mixing bowl	50–60 minutes
5 cup pudding basin	1 hour 10 minutes

Medium Madeira Cake

1 cup soft margarine or butter, at room temperature

1 cup superfine sugar

4 eggs

2 tablespoons milk

2½ cups self-rising flour

1 teaspoon baking powder (for roasting pan cake only)

FLAVORINGS

Vanilla 2 teaspoons vanilla extract

Lemon grated zest of 1 lemon; replace·milk with 2 tablespoons lemon juice

Orange grated zest of 1 orange; replace milk with 2 tablespoons orange juice

Chocolate replace ½ cup plus 2 tablespoons flour with same quantity of cocoa powder

The above amount will fill:

SIZE OF CONTAINER	BAKING TIME
12 x 9 x 2 inch roasting pan	30–35 minutes
6 cup pudding basin	1¼ –1½ hours
2 x 4 cup pudding basins	about 1 hour
5 cup and 3 cup pudding basins	1 hour 5 minutes – 1hour 10 minutes for larger basin cake, 55–60 minutes for smaller basin cake
8 inch single layer pan cake and 4 cup pudding basin	30 minutes for layer cake, about 1 hour for basin cake

Large Madeira Cake

1½ cups soft margarine or butter, at room temperature

1½ cups superfine sugar

6 eggs

4 tablespoons milk

5 cups self-rising flour

FLAVORINGS

Vanilla 3 teaspoons vanilla extract

Lemon grated zest of 2 lemons; replace milk with 4 tablespoons lemon juice

Orange grated zest of 2 oranges; replace milk with 4 tablespoons orange juice

Chocolate replace 1 cup flour with same quantity of cocoa powder

The above amount will fill:

SIZE OF CONTAINER	BAKING TIME
9 inch deep round cake pan	1–1¼ hours
8 inch deep square cake pan	1–1¼ hours

1 Cream the margarine or butter and sugar together in a bowl until light and fluffy. Beat the eggs and milk, or eggs only if you are making a fruit-flavored cake, in a small bowl with a fork. Mix the flour with the cocoa powder and baking powder, if using, in a separate small bowl. Add alternate spoonfuls of the egg mixture and flour and beat into the creamed mixture until they have all been incorporated and the cake mixture is smooth. Beat in the vanilla extract or grated lemon or orange zest and juice, if using.

2 Spoon the cake mixture into your chosen greased and lined pan. Bake in a preheated oven, 325°F, for the appropriate time (see boxed text), until well risen and golden brown and a cake tester comes out of the center of the cake cleanly (see page 19). Leave for 10 minutes in the pan, then loosen the edges with a spatula, turn out onto a wire rack and allow to cool completely.

QUICK-MIX CAKES

This is a quick and easy single-stage cake that can be made in minutes and may be used for varying-sized layer cakes and cupcakes. Quite simply, all the ingredients are put into the bowl at the same time and beaten for just a few minutes until smooth and creamy. If you are using butter, the secret is to have it at room temperature so that it will beat easily either with a wooden spoon, electric mixer, or food processor. As the mixing time is so brief, a little baking powder is added to boost the leavening agent in the self-rising flour and to guarantee success every time.

Large round Quick-mix Layer Cake

1 cup soft margarine

1 cup superfine sugar

2 cups self-rising flour

1 teaspoon baking powder

4 eggs

FLAVORINGS

Vanilla **1 teaspoon vanilla extract**

Lemon **grated zest of 1 lemon**

Orange **grated zest of 1 small orange**

Chocolate **replace 6 tablespoons flour with same quantity of cocoa powder**

1 Put all the ingredients into a bowl, with your chosen flavoring, if using, and beat together until smooth.

2 Spoon the cake mixture into 2 x 8 inch greased and base-lined layer pans (see page 11).

3 Bake in a preheated oven, 350°F, for about 25 minutes until springy to the touch (see page 19). Leave for 5 minutes in the pans, then turn out onto a wire rack and allow to cool completely.

Medium round Quick-mix Layer Cake

¾ cup soft margarine

¾ cup superfine sugar

1½ cups self-rising flour

½ teaspoon baking powder

3 eggs

FLAVORINGS

Vanilla ¾ **teaspoon vanilla extract**

Lemon **grated zest of ¾ lemon**

Orange **grated zest of ¾ small orange**

Chocolate **replace ¼ cup flour with same quantity of cocoa powder**

1 Put all the ingredients into a bowl, with your chosen flavoring, if using, and beat together until smooth.

2 Spoon the cake mixture into 2 x 7 inch greased and base-lined layer pans (see page 11).

3 Bake in a preheated oven, 350°F, for about 20 minutes until springy to the touch (see page 19). Leave for 5 minutes in the pans, then turn out onto a wire rack and allow to cool completely.

Small round Quick-mix Layer Cake

½ cup soft margarine

½ cup superfine sugar

1 cup self-rising flour

¼ teaspoon baking powder

2 eggs

FLAVORINGS

Vanilla ½ teaspoon vanilla extract

Lemon grated zest of ½ lemon

Orange grated zest of ½ small orange

Chocolate replace 2 tablespoons flour with the same quantity of cocoa powder

1 Put all the ingredients into a bowl, with your chosen flavoring, if using, and beat together until smooth.

2 Spoon the cake mixture into 2 x 6 inch greased and base-lined layer pans (see page 11).

3 Bake in a preheated oven, (350°F), for about 15 minutes until springy to the touch (see page 19). Leave for 5 minutes in the pans, then turn out onto a wire rack and allow to cool completely.

Tip

Some layer pans have slightly sloping sides. These are fine to use if the cake is just sandwiched together and topped with frosting, but if you plan to cover the sides of the cake with frosting, you will need straight-sided pans, otherwise the finished cake will have an unsatisfactory appearance.

Cupcakes
Makes 12

½ cup soft margarine

½ cup superfine sugar

1 cup self-rising flour

2 eggs

FLAVORINGS

Vanilla **½ teaspoon vanilla extract**

Lemon **grated zest of ½ lemon**

Orange **grated zest of ½ small orange**

Chocolate **replace 2 tablespoons flour with same quantity of cocoa powder**

1 Line a 12-section muffin pan with paper bake cups. Put all the ingredients into a bowl, with your chosen flavoring, if using, and beat together until smooth.

2 Divide the cake mixture evenly between the paper bake cups using a dessertspoon and level the surface.

3 Bake in a preheated oven, (350°F), for 15 minutes until springy to the touch (see page 19). Leave for 5 minutes in the pan, then remove cakes to a wire rack and allow to cool completely.

Shallow Cake

¼ cup soft margarine

¼ cup superfine sugar

½ cup self-rising flour

⅛ teaspoon baking powder

1 egg

1 Put all the ingredients into a bowl and beat together with a wooden spoon or an electric mixer until smooth.

2 Spoon into a 7 inch greased and base-lined layer pan (see page 11).

3 Bake in a preheated oven, 350°F, for 12–15 minutes until springy to the touch (see page 19). Leave for 5 minutes in the pan, then turn out onto a wire rack and allow to cool completely.

MUFFINS
Makes 12

2½ cups all-purpose flour

3 teaspoons baking powder

½ cup light brown sugar

3 eggs

4 tablespoons sunflower oil

¼ cup butter, melted

½ cup plain yogurt

FLAVORINGS

Vanilla **2 teaspoons vanilla extract**

Chocolate **replace 6 tablespoons flour with same quantity of cocoa powder**

Double chocolate **replace 6 tablespoons flour with same quantity of cocoa powder and add 4 oz diced milk chocolate**

1 Line a 12-section deep muffin pan with paper bake cups. Put all the ingredients into a bowl, with your chosen flavoring, if using, and combine with a fork until only just mixed.

2 Divide the muffin mixture evenly between the paper cups using a dessertspoon.

3 Bake the muffins in a preheated oven, 375°F, for 18–20 minutes until they are well risen and the tops are golden brown and have cracked slightly. Leave for 5 minutes in the pan, then remove cakes to a wire rack and allow to cool completely.

JELLY ROLL

Makes one 11 inch long jelly roll

4 large eggs

½ cup superfine sugar, plus extra for sprinkling

1 cup all-purpose flour

1 tablespoon hot water

8 tablespoons raspberry or strawberry jelly

FLAVORING

Chocolate **replace ¼ cup flour with the same quantity of cocoa powder and use chocolate spread in place of jelly**

1 Line a 15 x 11 inch roasting pan with nonstick parchment paper (see page 11), so that the paper stands about 1 inch high all around the sides. Put the eggs and sugar in a large heatproof bowl set over a saucepan of simmering water and beat, ideally using a hand-held electric beater, for about 10 minutes until very thick and pale and the mixture leaves a trail when the beater is lifted just above the bowl.

2 Sift in the flour and use a large metal spoon to fold it into the egg mixture, adding the measured water once most of the flour is incorporated.

3 Turn the cake mixture into the pan and ease gently into the corners. Bake in a preheated oven, 400°F, for 10–12 minutes until pale golden and just firm to the touch.

4 While the cake is baking, wet a clean dishtowel with hot water, wring it out and put on the work surface so that the short edges are facing you. Cover with a sheet of waxed paper and sprinkle evenly with sugar.

5 Turn the cake out onto the paper and peel off the lining paper. Spread the cake with the jelly, then roll up, starting from the short edge nearest to you. Put the jelly roll, seam side down, onto a wire rack to cool.

IS MY CAKE COOKED?

If your cake looks well risen and brown but you are not sure if it is ready, there are several methods of checking it. Insert a cake tester into the center of a deep cake. If it comes out cleanly, it is ready, but if there is a smearing of cake mixture, put the cake back in the oven and test again at five- or ten-minute intervals, depending on how messy the tester is.

For layer cakes and cupcakes, press the top of the cake lightly with a fingertip. If the cake springs back, then it is ready. If the finger mark remains, then return the cake to the oven and test again in five minutes' time.

All ovens vary slightly, so use the timings as a guide and check shortly before the end of the baking time to see how your cake or cakes are doing. Resist the temptation to keep opening the oven, especially midway through cooking, or your cake will sink. If you have a fan-assisted oven, adjust the temperature slightly and reduce by 25°F, because these ovens can run hot. For larger cakes, check two-thirds of the way through the baking time and cover the top loosely with foil if the cake is browning too quickly.

SLICING THE TOP OFF A CAKE

With the exception of layer cakes, most cakes tend to peak during cooking and will need trimming before frosting. The deeper the cake, the more it will rise in the center. Trim the top level using a large serrated knife and then turn large cakes upside down before frosting. Trim the tops of cupcakes if spooning over glacé icing so that it will form a flat even layer and not run off the cake.

SHORT OF TIME?

Cheat and buy a cake from the supermarket. With lots of flavored muffins, cupcakes, jelly rolls, and filled layer cakes to choose from, it can be a lifesaver for a busy working mom. Look out for thick slices of plain or marbled Madeira cake and sandwich three or four side by side to make a larger square cake. Larger bought round sponge cakes may be more difficult to find, so buy whatever size you can and just scale the design down and make a slightly smaller version.

Frostings and fillings

Some frostings—including butter frosting and ganache—are used as both a filling for a cake and as a delicious coating. Others, such as ready-to-use icing, are used only as a cake covering. Refer to the individual recipes for guidance.

READY-TO-USE ICING

For speed, most of us will opt to buy this icing from the supermarket, but if you would prefer to make your own, it really is very easy. If you can't find liquid glucose—it is usually sold alongside the vanilla extract and other flavorings in supermarkets—then order it from your local drugstore. Don't be tempted to leave it out, as it is crucial to the icing's elasticity. You will also find small boxes of dried egg white with the other baking ingredients in the supermarket, and, because it is pasteurized, it does not pose any potential health risk as in the case of raw egg white.

Makes 1 lb

1 dried egg white

2 tablespoons liquid glucose

4 cups confectioners' sugar, sifted

1 Reconstitute the egg white with water according to the package instructions.

2 Put the egg white into a large bowl with the liquid glucose, then gradually work in the sugar with a wooden spoon, kneading it with your hands straight onto the work surface when too stiff to stir. The mixture should be smooth and elastic, and you may find that you do not need to mix in all the sugar.

Tip

Ready-to-use icing dries out quickly, so make sure that it is tightly wrapped in a plastic bag until you are ready to use it.

BUTTER FROSTING

Sometimes known as buttercream, this is a soft spreading frosting that can be used plain or flavored, spread smooth or roughed up or even colored to fill and decorate cakes. For the best flavor, use good-quality unsalted butter at room temperature, or soften in the microwave, so that it is easy to mix with the confectioners' sugar. A newly opened pack of confectioners' sugar may be used straight from the pack, but if you have a pack that has been open a while, you may need to sift it before using to remove any lumps. Follow the method below and refer to the table for ingredient quantities and optional flavorings.

 Put the butter into a bowl and soften with a wooden spoon or beat in a food processor.

 Gradually beat in the sugar, then add the milk and/or your chosen flavoring, and mix to a soft spreading consistency.

QUANTITY	Single	One and a half	Double
unsalted butter, at room temperature	¼ cup	⅓ cup	½ cup
confectioners' sugar	1 cup	1½ cups	2 cups
milk	1 teaspoon	2 teaspoons	1 tablespoon
FLAVORINGS			
Vanilla	½ teaspoon vanilla extract	¾ teaspoon vanilla extract	1 teaspoon vanilla extract
Lemon	1 teaspoon grated lemon zest and 1 teaspoon lemon juice in place of milk	1½ teaspoons grated lemon zest and 2 teaspoons lemon juice in place of milk	2 teaspoons grated lemon zest and 1 tablespoon lemon juice in place of milk
Orange	1 teaspoon grated orange zest and 1 teaspoon orange juice in place of milk	1½ teaspoons grated orange zest and 2 teaspoons orange juice in place of milk	2 teaspoons grated orange zest and 1 tablespoon orange juice in place of milk
Chocolate	4 teaspoons cocoa powder dissolved in 2 teaspoons boiling water in place of milk	2 tablespoons cocoa powder dissolved in 4 teaspoons boiling water in place of milk	8 teaspoons cocoa powder dissolved in 2 tablespoons boiling water in place of milk

CHOCOLATE FUDGE FROSTING

This dark frosting thickens as it cools, so if you get delayed and the frosting has set too much to spread, beat in a little boiling water. This quantity will cover a 7 inch deep round or 6 inch deep square Small Madeira Cake (see page 12).

2 tablespoons butter

2 tablespoons cocoa powder

1½ cups confectioners' sugar (no need to sift)

2 tablespoons milk

pinch of ground cinnamon (optional)

1   Melt the butter in a small saucepan over a low heat. Stir in the cocoa powder and cook over a medium heat, stirring constantly, for 30 seconds until smooth.

2   Remove from the heat and gradually stir in the sugar and milk, mixing until smooth. Mix in the ground cinnamon, if using.

3   Return to the heat and cook for 1 minute, stirring constantly, until the frosting has a glossy pouring consistency. Quickly spread over the cake while the frosting is still warm.

GLOSSY CHOCOLATE BUTTER FROSTING

A rich, dark, shiny frosting made with a mixture of dark and milk chocolate so that it is full of flavor but without the bitterness of dark chocolate that children dislike. This quantity will cover a 9 inch deep round or 8 inch deep square Medium Madeira Cake (see page 13).

¼ cup butter

4 oz good-quality milk chocolate

4 oz good-quality dark chocolate

½ cup confectioners' sugar (no need to sift)

2 tablespoons milk

1   Melt the butter in a small saucepan over a low heat. Break the chocolate into pieces, add to the pan and heat gently, stirring occasionally, until just melted.

2   Remove from the heat and stir in the sugar and the milk. Return to the heat, if necessary, stirring constantly, until the frosting is smooth and glossy. Use immediately.

Tip
As an alternative, this frosting could be flavored with a little finely grated orange zest or instant coffee powder.

DOUBLE CHOCOLATE GANACHE

This is a rich creamy frosting made with warmed cream and half dark and half milk chocolate. It will set as it cools, so it is best to make it about 1 hour before you need it. This amount will cover a 7 inch deep round or 6 inch deep square Small Madeira Cake (see page 12). For a larger quantity, use 1¼ cups heavy cream and 10 oz chocolate.

¾ cup heavy cream

4 oz good-quality milk chocolate

4 oz good-quality dark chocolate

1 Heat the cream in a small saucepan over a medium heat until it is almost boiling and just beginning to bubble around the edges.

2 Remove the pan from the heat, break the chocolate into pieces and add to the pan. Set aside for 10 minutes or so, stirring occasionally, until the chocolate has melted.

3 Cover with plastic wrap, allow to cool then chill in the refrigerator for 30 minutes–1 hour until thickened enough to hold its shape. The time will vary depending on how hot the cream was.

Tip

If you get delayed and the frosting chills for longer, soften it once more by standing the basin in a saucepan of just-boiled water for a minute or two. Stir before using.

WHITE CHOCOLATE CREAM

Deliciously chocolaty, this cream can be used to fill and cover a 7 inch deep round vanilla- or chocolate-flavored Small Madeira Cake (see page 12) or a 9 inch deep round Medium Madeira Cake (see page 13), cut into 8 individual cakes using a 2½ inch plain cookie cutter or upturned tumbler as a template using a small serrated knife, as for the White Chocolate Treats on page 93.

6 oz white chocolate

1¼ cups heavy cream

1 Break the chocolate into pieces and put in a heatproof bowl set over a half-filled saucepan of just-boiled water. Set aside for 5 minutes, off the heat, until the chocolate has melted.

2 Whip the cream in a large bowl until it forms soft swirls. Stir the melted chocolate, then gently fold into the cream. Use immediately.

GLACÉ ICING

A quick-to-make, spoonable icing that can be used plain or colored. If your child has adventurous tastes, try replacing the water with orange or lemon juice. This quantity will cover 12 Cupcakes (see page 16).

1½ cups confectioners' sugar, sifted

3–4 teaspoons water

1 Sift the sugar into a medium bowl, pressing the last grains through the strainer with the back of a spoon.

2 Gradually stir in just enough of the measurement water to mix to a smooth thick icing that will flow from a spoon.

ROYAL ICING

Most often used to decorate wedding and Christmas cakes, here royal icing is also used to pipe on cake details or to stick icing decorations in place. Royal icing sets hard as it dries, so if making it in advance, cover the surface closely with plastic wrap, stir before using and loosen the mixture with a few drops of lemon juice, if necessary.

1 dried egg white

2 cups confectioners' sugar, sifted

1 Reconstitute the egg white with water according to the package instructions.

2 Gradually beat in the sugar a tablespoon or so at a time until the icing forms soft peaks that hold their shape. You may find that you do not need to add all the sugar.

Tip
Dried egg white is generally sold in small envelopes that are the equivalent to two egg whites—make sure that you use only half an envelope.

Techniques

The individual cake designs in this book detail the specific techniques involved in frosting and decorating the cakes, but the following are the basic techniques that are routinely used.

USING READY-TO-USE ICING

Ready-to-use icing may be sold plain white, in ivory or in a variety of pastel and vibrant colors ranging from pale lilac, pink, and blue to cerise pink, turquoise, orange or purple, and the deepest red or black. Whether you choose to buy white and color your own with food colorings (see below) or buy ready colored, the icing should be kneaded on a surface lightly dusted with a little sifted confectioners' sugar to soften it slightly before rolling. Any icing that you are not going to use immediately must be tightly wrapped in a plastic bag or plastic wrap so that it does not dry out.

FOOD COLORINGS

These can be used to color ready-to-use icing, royal icing, and butter frosting, as well as shredded coconut. They are most often sold in paste or liquid form and are very concentrated, so add them cautiously. For very intense, deep colors, opt for paste colorings. Reserve liquid colorings for creating pastel shades of icing, as the more of these you add, the stickier your icing can become, especially when using ready-to-use icing. Add dots of coloring from the tip of a toothpick and gradually build up the color until you achieve the desired shade, kneading well between additions. You can always add a little extra, but once added, the only way to reduce the color is to mix with more icing. Sometimes a marbled effect is required. In this case, only partially mix in the coloring, then roll out for a color-veined finish.

CHOOSING A CAKE BOARD

Traditionally, birthday cakes were always served on thick or thin foil-covered cake boards, but now with such a wide choice of colored chinaware and other items and materials on offer, you may prefer to serve your cake on a china plate, a colored wood, glass, or a plastic cutting board.

COVERING A CAKE BOARD WITH READY-TO-USE ICING

1 Spread a little butter frosting or jelly thinly along the edge or edges of the cake board top.

2 Knead the ready-to-use icing on a surface lightly dusted with sifted confectioners' sugar until slightly softened. Lightly dust a rolling pin with confectioners' sugar, then roll out the icing to a round or square a little larger (about ½ inch) all around than the board, moving the icing and redusting the work surface lightly with confectioners' sugar as needed.

3 Lift the icing on the rolling pin and drape it over the board. Smooth in place with your fingertips dusted with confectioners' sugar.

4 Lift the board and trim off the excess icing around the edge or edges with a small knife.

5 Re-knead the icing trimmings, tightly wrap in a plastic bag or plastic wrap and reserve.

Tip
For larger cake boards, you may find it easier to roll the icing straight onto the cake board lightly dusted with confectioners' sugar with a rolling pin.

COVERING A CAKE WITH READY-TO-USE ICING

1 Put the cake on the cake board or plate and spread the top and side or sides thinly with butter frosting or apricot jelly.

2 Knead the ready-to-use icing on a surface lightly dusted with sifted confectioners' sugar. Lightly dust a rolling pin with confectioners' sugar, then roll out the icing to a round or square about 5 inches larger in diameter than the cake top. Lift the icing on the rolling pin and drape over the cake.

3 Ease the icing over the sides of the cake, smoothing it with your fingertips dusted with confectioners' sugar. As the icing is so pliable, you should be able to shape it without any creases.

4 Trim away the excess icing from the base of the board or plate with a small knife. Using the palms of your hands dusted with confectioners' sugar, smooth out any bumps, making the surface as flat as you can.

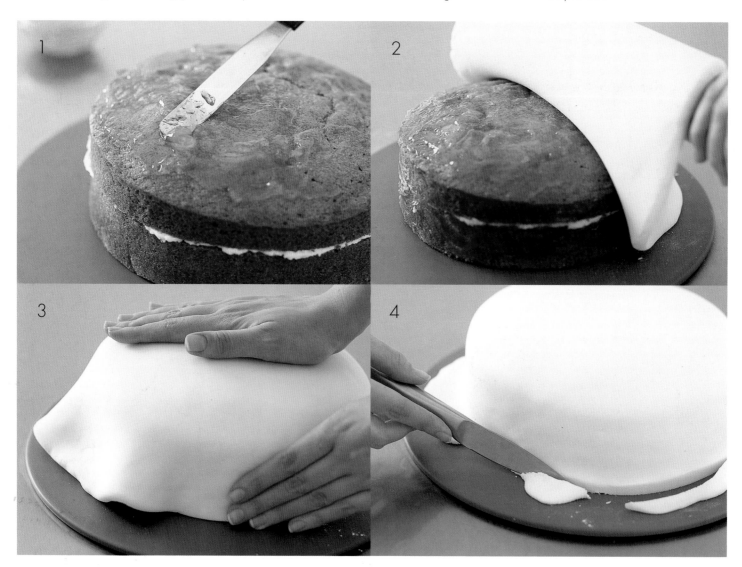

DECORATING A CAKE BOARD WITH AN ICING BORDER

Instead of covering a cake board with icing, you can add a border of icing to the cake board edge or edges once the cake has been decorated. Cut one long strip of rolled-out icing and join at the back of a round cake or cut strips the same length as the board sides of a square board and trim the ends diagonally so that the edges can be butted together neatly.

COVERING A CAKE WITH BUTTER FROSTING

1 Put the sandwiched cake onto a cake board or plate, then spread a little butter frosting very thinly over the top and side or sides of the cake to stick the crumbs in place.

2 Spread a more generous layer of butter frosting over the top and side or sides of the cake, smoothing in place with a small spatula.

Finishing touches

This is the fun, creative part! But do not be nervous if you are a novice at cake decorating. There are lots of inventive ways of using basic cut-out icing shapes, candies, and chocolates to add novelty and decorative details to your cakes with the minimum of time.

PIPED ICING

Tubes of ready-made icing with small detachable plastic piping tips are sold in most supermarkets, as are smaller tubes of writing icing, which are ideal when only tiny amounts of piping are needed. Where larger amounts are required, you may prefer to use homemade royal icing (see page 25) and spoon it into a waxed paper pastry bag. These are easy to make and you can simply snip off the tip to pipe the icing or use a piping tip.

CUTTING OUT ICING SHAPES

Stamping out shapes with cutters is a quick and easy way for even the most inexperienced at cake icing to decorate a cake. Cutters can be used to create hearts and stars, circles and triangles, numbers and flowers. Add the shapes immediately to the cake or leave to dry and prop up at angles on a dot of piped icing for an extra dimension.

Using plunger cutters offers a fail-safe way of stamping out tiny shapes, as the plunger gently pushes the icing shape out of the cutter easily every time.

Metal piping tips can be used in a variety of ways to cut out shapes. The ends of large cream plain piping tips, either ⅜ inch, ¼ inch, or ½ inch, can be used to cut out small rounds as well as larger rounds using the upturned ends. Small piping tips can be used to cut out tiny rounds, again using the upturned end.

To create crescent moon shapes, cut out rounds with cookie cutters or piping tips, then use the same cutter or tip to cut partially into each round to cut a crescent shape.

Shapes do not need to be solid. Try cutting a smaller shape from a larger one to make heart, star, or circle frames, then leave empty or fill with a second colored shape.

HOW TO MAKE A PASTRY BAG

1 Cut a 10 inch square of waxed paper and fold in half to make a large triangle. Fold the triangle in half through the folded edge and pinch the second folded edge to mark the central fold.

2 Open out again. Holding the center of the long folded edge toward you, curl the left-hand point of the triangle over to meet the center pinch mark, forming a cone.

3 Next, bring the right-hand point over and around the cone so that the 3 points meet.

4 Lastly, fold the top points down several times to prevent the paper cone from unraveling.

TO USE THE BAG

Half-fill the bag with icing, fold the top edge down to enclose the icing, then snip off the end. Make only a tiny snip, then squeeze out a little icing. Enlarge the hole with scissors if the piping needs to be larger. If using a metal piping tip, snip off the end and drop the tip into the bag, enlarging the hole if needed so that it fits snugly with half the tip showing, then half-fill the bag with icing. For larger piping tips, use a reusable fabric or plastic bag with a ready-cut end.

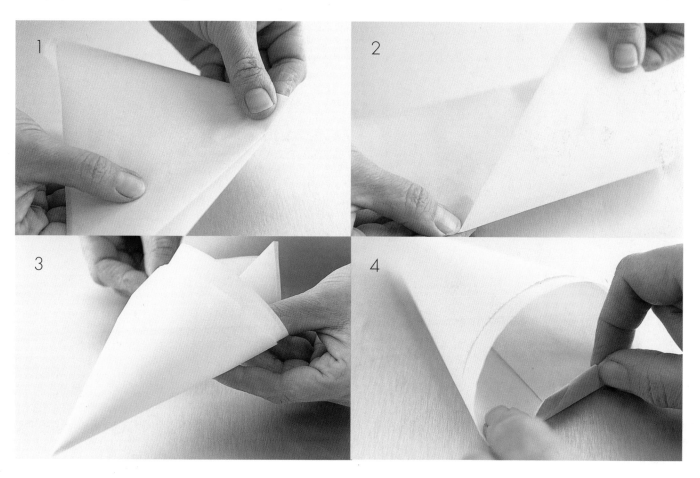

MAKING FLOWERS

Specialty cake-decorating stores sell a great range of fancy-shaped cutters, but you can easily be swept away with the choice. Try to go for shapes that you will use more than once, such as a set of different-size flower plunger cutters or daisy cutters, rather than a single complicated orchid or rose.

To give added shape to flowers, press the flower out of the plunger cutter onto a piece of foam—a new foam washing-up sponge is ideal. This will curl the edges of the petals. Alternatively, curl the flowers on pieces of crumpled nonstick parchment paper set in a muffin pan. Once the flowers have been shaped, transfer them to a baking sheet lined with nonstick parchment paper to harden.

If, when cutting flowers, the icing sticks to the cutter, then dip the cutter into a little confectioners' sugar between use.

MAKING CHOCOLATE CURLS

These always look effective and are very simple to make, especially if the chocolate is at room temperature.

1 Turn a bar of chocolate over so that the smooth underside is uppermost. Position on the edge of a work surface.

2 Using a swivel-bladed vegetable peeler, pare away thin shavings of chocolate from the bar. If the curls are very small, warm the chocolate in a microwave oven for 10–15 seconds on High (if 650 watt) or Medium (if 700 watt) and try again.

3 For smaller, finer curls, grate the chocolate onto a plate instead using a medium or small grater setting.

WRAPPING CAKES WITH CHOCOLATE

This eye-catching but easy decoration is made by spreading melted chocolate onto a strip of nonstick parchment paper that is a little taller than the side of your cake and long enough to wrap right around the outside of the cake. The secret is to melt the chocolate gently so that it stays glossy.

1 Bring a saucepan of water to a boil then set a large heatproof bowl over it so that it will heat up but not touch the water. Break the chocolate into the bowl, then remove the pan from the heat and leave for 5 minutes until the chocolate has melted.

2 Stir, then spread the chocolate over the strip of paper right up to one long edge and then make a wavy, jagged, or swirly edge a little way down from the opposite long edge.

3 Press the chocolate onto the side of the cake so that the paper is on the outside, the soft chocolate is pressed against the cake and the decorative edge is uppermost.

4 Chill until set, then peel away the paper. Decorate the side of the cake with ribbon, if desired.

USING CANDIES AND CHOCOLATES

Adding brightly colored candies or chocolates to cakes creates maximum impact for minimum effort. These items can easily be used to give the effect of eyeballs (see page 36), spots (see page 90), jewels (see page 50), spider legs (see page 132), whiskers (see page 62), or simple lines of color (see page 80).

USING CANDLES

For very young children, it just wouldn't be a birthday cake without a candle to mark each year of their age. Look out for pastel- or primary-colored ones, dotty or glittery ones, shaped, wiggly or wand-like ones, numerical candles, those that spell "happy birthday," or even those that will not blow out! Add candles to candleholders to catch the melting wax or make your own with tiny balls or shapes of ready-to-use icing.

Tiny tots

Cheeky pirate

serves 10
decoration time 1 hour

double quantity Butter Frosting (see page 21)

pink paste food coloring

Large round Quick-mix Layer Cake
   (see page 14)

9 inch thin round cake board or plate

8 oz red ready-to-use icing

sifted confectioners' sugar, for dusting

3 oz white ready-to-use icing

1 round blue licorice candy

2 oz royal blue ready-to-use icing

1 oz black ready-to-use icing

1 gold foil-covered coin

Tip

The bandanna colors can be varied
according to the colors of icing that you
happen to have. For example, use a
combination of blue, green, and white,
or green, yellow, and brown.

1 Color the butter frosting pale pink with the coloring, then use some of the frosting to sandwich the cakes together. Put onto the cake board or plate. Reserve 2 teaspoons of the butter frosting and spread the remainder over the top and side of the cake, smoothing with a small spatula.

2 Knead the red icing on a surface lightly dusted with confectioners' sugar until slightly softened. Roll out until a little larger than half the cake top. Cut a straight edge with a knife. Drape the icing over the cake so that the cut edge covers one-third of the cake top in a diagonal line, draping downward on the right-hand side of the cake to the cake board, and add a few pleats to resemble a bandanna. Trim off the excess.

3 Re-knead and roll out the trimmings. Cut out a mouth shape and 2 very thin strips for the ends of the mouth and press in place on the cake.

4 Knead and roll out the white icing. Cut out small rounds using the upturned end of a piping tip and press these at intervals onto the bandanna, sticking them in place with a little water. Roll a small white icing ball, then flatten, shape into an oval eye and press onto the pirate's face. Add the blue candy for the eyeball and stick in place with a tiny dot of the reserved butter frosting. Color the remaining white icing pale pink with the coloring and shape into an ear. Press onto the side of the cake.

5 Knead and roll out the blue icing. Cut out more spots for the bandanna. Knead and roll out the black icing. Cut out a semicircle for an eyepatch. Shape the remaining black icing into a thin rope and press above the eyepatch, across the face and over the ear. Add a gold coin earring and stick in place with a dot of butter frosting.

King of the road

serves 20
decoration time 45 minutes

1 Trim the top of the cake level, if needed. Cut the cake horizontally in half, then sandwich back together with most of the butter frosting. Put onto the cake board or plate. Spread the top and side very thinly with the remaining butter frosting.

2 Cut off 8 oz of the white icing, wrap and reserve. Knead the remaining icing, roll out and use to cover the top and sides of the cake and the cake board. Smooth with the fingertips, trim off the excess and wrap the trimmings.

3 Color the 8 oz reserved white icing pale gray with a little of the black coloring. Shape three-quarters of the gray into a long rope 18 inches long, then flatten it into a strip 1½ inches wide with a rolling pin. Straighten one long edge, then cut the opposite edge into a wavy line. Position around the lower side of the cake, wavy edge uppermost, sticking it in place with a little water, if necessary. Trim off the excess. Knead and roll out the reserved gray icing and cut out a winding road and stick onto the cake top with a little water. Color the trimmings black, wrap and reserve.

4 Knead and roll out the red icing and cut out 2 cars 3 inches long. Knead and roll out the blue icing and cut out 2 trucks of similar size. Press onto the cake, leaving space for the yellow cars. Knead and roll out a little yellow icing, cut out 2 cars and press into the spaces. Roll small black balls then flatten for wheels. Press onto the cars, sticking in place with water.

5 Shape a larger 3-D car from the remaining yellow icing and position on the road, standing on pieces of icing trimmings, then cover these with black wheels. Roll out the white icing trimmings, cut out small shapes for car windows and add. Roll small balls and press on for headlights. Add tiny white strips for road markings. Cut very thin strips from any remaining red and black icing, trim and press onto the large yellow car hood and trunk. Add lollipop road signs.

9 inch deep round Large Madeira Cake (see page 13)

one-and-a-half quantity Butter Frosting (see page 21)

11 inch thin round cake board or plate

1 lb 8 oz white ready-to-use icing

sifted confectioners' sugar, for dusting

black paste food coloring

3 oz red ready-to-use icing

3 oz blue ready-to-use icing

6 oz yellow ready-to-use icing

2 red lollipops, unwrapped

Tips

- For a child who may be getting a toy race track for a birthday present, use a little more gray icing and make it into a circular roadway on top of the cake.
- Use any remaining icing trimmings to make additional road signs by covering toothpicks with ropes of icing then adding flattened balls of colored icing. Leave to dry flat on nonstick parchment paper, then pipe on details—perhaps the child's age or name—with tubes of writing icing.

Magic numbers

serves 8
decoration time 45 minutes

7 inch deep round Small Madeira Cake
   (see page 12)

single quantity Butter Frosting (see page 21)

8 inch thin round cake board or plate

14 oz white ready-to-use icing

sifted confectioners' sugar, for dusting

blue paste food coloring

4 oz yellow ready-to-use icing

4 oz red ready-to-use icing

4 oz orange ready-to-use icing

Tips
- Adjust the sum to relate to the age of the particular individual—this is a great cake for all ages, including bigger birthdays such as 18, 40, or even 80!
- Boxed sets of small number cutters can be bought from good cookware stores, cookware departments in large department stores, or specialty cake-decorating stores.

1 Cut the cake horizontally in half, then sandwich back together with most of the butter frosting. Put onto the cake board or plate. Spread the top and side very thinly with the remaining butter frosting.

2 Knead the white icing on a surface lightly dusted with confectioners' sugar until slightly softened. Roll out and use to cover the cake. Smooth in place with your fingertips dusted with confectioners' sugar, then trim off the excess.

3 Color the trimmings bright blue with the food coloring and knead until an even color. Wrap and reserve.

4 Knead and roll out a little of the yellow icing and cut out a number 2 and different-size stars with small cutters. Knead and roll out some red icing and cut out a number 3 and some stars. Knead and roll out some of the orange icing and cut out some number 5s and some stars.

5 Arrange the yellow 2, the red 3, and one orange 5 on top of the cake, leaving spaces in between. Stick colored stars randomly over the cake top with a little water.

6 Roll out the reserved blue icing, cut some small narrow strips and press onto the cake top between the numbers for plus and equals signs. Stamp out a few tiny stars and press onto the cake top, then cut out large stars from the remaining blue.

7 Stick the large blue stars around the side of the cake, leaving spaces in between for numbers. Add alternate-colored 5s to the spaces, using the orange 5s you cut out earlier and re-kneading and rolling out the rest of the icing trimmings to cut 5s from other colors, as necessary.

Alien invasion

serves 6
decoration time 45 minutes

6 Muffins (see page 17) or bought large
    muffins, paper cups removed

single quantity vanilla-flavored Butter Frosting
    (see page 21)

selection of licorice or fruit candies

5 oz bright pink ready-to-use icing

sifted confectioners' sugar, for dusting

large round plate

5 oz blue ready-to-use icing

5 oz green ready-to-use icing

2 black licorice "wheels"

1 Stand the muffins on a cutting board and spread the butter
frosting over the tops and sides to cover. Press on the licorice
or fruit candies for eyes and noses.

2 Knead the pink icing on a surface lightly dusted with
confectioners' sugar until slightly softened. Roll out thinly and
cut narrow strips. Drape the strips randomly over the tops of
2 muffins so that they cover the butter frosting and extend
down and over the work surface. Carefully transfer to a large
round plate.

3 Repeat with each of the remaining pieces of different-colored
icing until each of the 6 muffins has been covered with the
different-colored strips.

4 To complete, press pieces of unwound licorice "wheel" into
the top of the muffins for antennae.

Tip
Let your imagination run riot and add
whacky colored feet, mouths, or ears
made out of icing or candies.

High flyer

serves 12
decoration time 1 hour

12 x 9 x 2 inch roasting pan Medium Madeira
    Cake (see page 13)

one-and-a-half quantity Butter Frosting
    (see page 21)

10 x 14 inch rectangular cake board, covered
    with 1 lb pale blue ready-to-use icing, or
    similar-size glass cutting board

1 lb white ready-to-use icing

sifted confectioners' sugar, for dusting

12 oz red ready-to-use icing

3 oz gray ready-to-use icing

2 black and white licorice candies, 1 halved,
    1 quartered

Tips

• Although this design is for a young
  child, the colors could be changed
  and easily adapted to make a Spitfire,
  Mosquito, or other plane for a model-
  making enthusiast. Borrow the kit box
  for reference for the correct colors
  and markings.
• If the licorice candies are too heavy to
  stick, use the remaining butter frosting
  from the edge of the bowl as glue.

1 Put the cake top downwards on a cutting board with a narrow edge nearest you. Cut a 5 inch strip the length of the longest side for the plane body. Cut the remaining piece in half through the longest edge. Reserve one piece for wings. Cut a ¾ inch strip off the side of the remaining piece. Reserve for the top tail fin. Put the last piece onto the plane body and shape into the cockpit, rounding off the front, tapering the back and sides and sloping the roof. Curve the edges of the plane.

2 Cut the reserved wing cake horizontally in half to form 2 thinner wings. Shape the tips and cut a slim diagonal slice off the other side to fit against the body of the plane.

3 Stick all the plane body parts together with butter frosting, keeping the wings and tail fin separate. Spread the outside thinly with butter frosting, then the wings and tail fin. Lift the body onto the cake or cutting board to sit diagonally.

4 Knead and roll out the white icing to 13 x 9 inches, drape over the cake and smooth in place. Trim off the excess. Re-knead, roll out and cover the top tail fin. Cut the side tail detail from the icing trimmings and stick in place with water.

5 Knead and roll out one-third of the red icing and cut 2 strips 12 x 1 inch then press around the base of the plane, fitting up to the side tail detail and front nose cone. Cut a curved strip for the nose cone and stick in place. Use the remaining red icing to cover the wings. Place them against the plane body. Cut the top tail fin details from the trimmings.

6 Knead and roll out the gray icing and cut a semicircle for the front window and round side windows and stick in place. Cut strips for the wing and fin details. Stick 2 candy quarters in front of each wing and a halved candy to each side of the tail.

space ship

serves 10
decoration time 1 hour

1 Cut the layer cake horizontally in half. Level the basin cake top, if necessary, then cut horizontally in half. Sandwich both cakes back together with some of the butter frosting. Spread the top of the layer cake with some of the butter frosting and put the basin cake, trimmed top downward, on top.

2 Transfer the cake stack to the smaller cake board and spread the remaining butter frosting thinly all over the top and sides.

3 Knead the white icing on a surface lightly dusted with confectioners' sugar until slightly softened. Roll out to a 12 inch round. Lift over the cake with a rolling pin, smooth in place and trim off the excess. Stand the cake stack on a saucer or lid on the icing-covered larger cake board or plate so that it is raised slightly above it.

4 Reknead and roll out the icing trimmings. Cut out tiny stars with a mini cutter. Cut out rounds in 2 sizes using the upturned end of a small- and medium-size piping tip, then cut part way through the larger rounds to create crescent moon shapes. Add the flying saucer candies to the board or plate, reserving one.

5 Stick the round blue licorice candies and white chocolate buttons alternately around the side of the bottom cake with piped dots of royal or writing icing.

6 Stick the green twisted bootlaces around the base of the top cake with piped dots of icing. Stick candy-covered chocolate drops above, adding 2 blue, then a green. Stick gummy candies in a line above, adding 2 orange, then a green.

7 Decorate the top of the space ship with lollipops. Add the reserved flying saucer, with the square licorice candy and an offcut of bootlace, cut side uppermost, on top, securing with piped dots of royal or writing icing.

Large single Quick-mix layer cake (see page 14) and 4 cup pudding basin Medium Madeira Cake (see page 13)

one-and-a-half-quantity Butter Frosting (see page 21)

8 inch thin round cake board

1 lb white ready-to-use icing

sifted confectioners' sugar, for dusting

saucer or jelly jar lid

12 inch thin round cake board, covered with 12 oz deep blue ready-to-use icing, or a large blue plate

flying saucer sherbet candies

14 round blue and 1 square orange licorice candies

14 white chocolate rainbow buttons

2 tablespoons Royal Icing (see page 25) or 1 tube white writing icing

4 green apple-flavored twisted bootlaces, cut to short lengths

20 blue and 11 green candy-covered chocolate drops

7 mixed lime green, yellow, and orange lollipops

18 orange and 10 green gummy candies

Tip

Vary the candies according to your child's particular preferences. Look out for fruity versions of licorice candies too.

Knight's castle

serves 24
decoration time 1 hour

8 inch deep square chocolate-flavored Large
   Madeira Cake (see page 13)

one-and-a-half quantity chocolate-flavored Butter
   Frosting (see page 21)

10 inch thin square cake board, covered with
   8 oz black ready-to-use icing, or plate

2 lb white ready-to-use icing

sifted confectioners' sugar, for dusting

black paste food coloring

11 inch chocolate-flavored Jelly Roll (see page
   18) or 9 inch bought chocolate jelly roll

13 oz deep blue ready-to-use icing

little Royal Icing (see page 25), colored gray

little Royal Icing (see page 25), colored black or
   tube black writing icing

4 chocolate sticks

1 oz yellow ready-to-use icing

1 oz green ready-to-use icing

Tips

- If you are short of time, then use bought toothpick flags for the pennants on the turret tops.
- If you choose to bake your own jelly roll for this cake from the recipe on page 18 you will find you have quite a bit to spare after making the turrets and gate tower. This can be eaten as a cook's perk!

1 Trim the top of the cake level, if needed. Cut the cake horizontally in half and sandwich back together with some of the butter frosting. Reserve 4 tablespoons of the butter frosting and spread the remainder thinly over the top and sides. Place on the cake board or plate.

2 Knead the white icing, then color gray with the black coloring until partially mixed and mottled.

3 Wrap and reserve 5 oz of the gray icing. Use the remainder to cover the cake. Trim off the excess and reserve.

4 Cut the jelly roll into four 2 inch thick slices for turrets and one 1 inch thick slice. Cut the latter in half and use one half for the gate tower. Spread the top and sides of the jelly roll pieces with most of the remaining butter frosting.

5 Roll out the remaining gray icing in batches. Cut four 2½ inch plain rounds with a cookie cutter and press onto the turret tops. Cut four 2 x 9 inch pieces and cover the turret sides. Cover the gate tower with a smaller piece. Reserve any trimmings. Stick the jelly roll pieces in place with the last of the butter frosting.

6 Knead and shape half the blue icing into a rope ¾ inch thick. Cut into ¾ inch wide slices and cut every other one in half. Stick these alternate-sized "bricks" around the fort top and the turret tops with a little piped gray royal icing. Repeat until all the top edges are covered. Cut a blue door from the trimmings. Stick onto the fort front.

7 Color the remaining gray ready-to-use icing black. Roll out, cut large and smaller squares. Stick around the door and corners of the castle with gray piped icing. Pipe on a black portcullis. Press chocolate sticks into the turrets. Roll out the yellow and green ready-to-use icing, cut flags and attach.

Fairy princess crowns

serves 12
decoration time 45 minutes, plus drying

single quantity Butter Frosting (see page 21)

pink paste food coloring

12 Cupcakes (see page 16) or bought
cupcakes, paper cups removed

1 lb pale pink ready-to-use icing

sifted confectioners' sugar, for dusting

mauve sugar sprinkles

blue and pink icing shapes

red gummy diamonds

1 tube fine white or pink writing icing or little
Royal Icing (see page 25)

large round or square plate

1 Color the butter frosting pale pink with the food coloring.
Trim the tops of cakes level, if needed, then turn each cake
top downward and spread the butter frosting over the new
tops and sides.

2 Knead the pink ready-to-use icing on a surface lightly dusted
with confectioners' sugar until slightly softened. Roll out one-
third and cut 3 strips 8 x 2 inches long. Using the upturned
end of a large cream plain piping tip, cut a scalloped
edge along one of the long edges. Repeat on the other
2 icing strips.

3 Press an icing strip, scalloped edge uppermost, around one
cake to form a crown, trimming off the excess and reserving.
Press the tips of the crown upright—if they are very floppy,
trim a little off the tips. Use the trimmings to make a fourth
crown then continue with the remaining icing. Repeat until all
12 crowns have been made.

4 Spoon the mauve sprinkles inside each crown, then decorate
the sides with icing shapes and gummy diamonds, sticking
them in place with dots of piped writing or royal icing.
Transfer the crowns to a plate. Leave for 30 minutes in a cool
place for the icing to harden.

Tip

Look out for tubs of different-colored
sprinkles and tiny sugar decorations.
Each tub is divided into five or six sections,
each containing a toning sprinkle or icing
sugar decoration.

Daisy chain

serves 10
decoration time 1 hour, plus drying

Large round Quick-mix Layer Cake
(see page 14)

single quantity Butter Frosting (see page 21)

10 inch thin round cake board, covered with
12 oz white ready-to-use icing, or plate

1 lb pale yellow ready-to-use icing

sifted confectioners' sugar, for dusting

vegetable shortening, for greasing

2 oz white flower paste (see tip, below)

3 tablespoons Royal Icing (see page 25),
colored pale green

1 tablespoon Royal Icing (see page 25),
colored yellow, or 1 tube yellow writing
icing

36 inches x ¾ inch wide pale green chiffon
ribbon

Tips
• Make sure that you bake the cakes in
straight-sided rather than sloping pans
for a smooth-sided finish.
• Flower paste can be bought from
specialty cake-decorating stores and can
be rolled very much more thinly than
ordinary ready-to-use icing.

1 Sandwich the cakes together with some of the butter frosting.
Transfer to the cake board or plate. Reserve 1 teaspoon of
the butter frosting and spread the remainder thinly over the
top and side of the cake.

2 Knead the yellow ready-to-use icing on a surface lightly
dusted with confectioners' sugar until slightly softened. Roll out
and use to cover the cake. Smooth the top and side with your
fingers dusted with confectioners' sugar. Trim off the excess.

3 To make the flowers, rub a little vegetable shortening over a
cutting board, rolling pin and base of a 1 inch and ¾ inch
plastic daisy cutter. Cut off half the flower paste, wrap and
reserve. Roll out the remaining flower paste thinly. Stamp out
a few flower shapes at a time and lift off the board with a
small knife onto pieces of crumpled nonstick parchment
paper to shape. Allow to dry for 30 minutes. Continue
stamping, re-kneading and rolling out the trimmings, and
using the reserved flower paste, until it has all been used up.

4 Spoon the pale green royal icing into a waxed paper pastry
bag (see page 31), snip off the end and pipe a swirly line
over the top and slightly over the side of the cake for a daisy
stem. Stick the flowers at intervals over the piped stem,
adding some to the base of the cake board with dots of
green piped icing.

5 Pipe dots of yellow icing in the centers of the flowers. Tie the
ribbon in a bow around the side of the cake and trim off the
excess ribbon.

Sunflower cupcakes

serves 12
decoration time 30 minutes

1 Trim the tops of the cupcakes level, if needed. Divide the butter frosting between the tops of the cakes then spread into an even layer.

2 Knead the yellow icing on a surface lightly dusted with confectioners' sugar until slightly softened. Roll out and cut into 1 inch wide strips. Cut each strip into triangular-shaped petals and stick around the edge of each cake.

3 Add a second row of icing petals, a little in from the first, re-rolling the trimmings as needed. Knead and roll out the brown icing and cut out 1 inch circles with a fluted cutter. Press into the center of each flower.

4 Pipe on red mouths and black eyes with writing icing. Arrange the cakes on the plate.

single quantity Butter Frosting (see page 21)

12 Cupcakes (see page 16), with green foil paper cups

8 oz yellow ready-to-use icing

sifted confectioners' sugar, for dusting

4 oz brown ready-to-use icing

1 tube red writing icing

1 tube black writing icing

large green plate

Tip
Chocolate candies or jumbo chocolate buttons could be used for the flower faces, if preferred.

Mini birthday cakes

serves 12
decoration time 20 minutes, plus drying

single quantity Glacé Icing (see page 24)

mauve paste food coloring

pink or red paste food coloring

yellow paste food coloring

12 Cupcakes (see page 16), with white paper
    cups, or bought cupcakes

4 each of yellow and white, pink, mauve and
    white candles

3 oz dolly mixture candies

3 oz candy-covered chocolate drops

large round or square plate

1 Put one-third of the glacé icing into a separate bowl and color lilac with a little mauve coloring. Spoon half the remaining icing into another bowl and color pale pink with the pink coloring or with a little of the red coloring. Color the remaining icing pale yellow.

2 Spoon the yellow icing over 4 of the cupcakes, the lilac icing over another 4 and the pink icing over the remaining cakes, smoothing in place with the back of the spoon.

3 Add a yellow and white candle to the center of each yellow iced cake, then press coordinating-colored candies around the base of each candle. Repeat with the correspondingly colored candles and candies for the remaining cakes. Transfer the cakes to a plate. Leave in a cool place for the icing to set for 30 minutes before serving.

Tip

For chocolate fans, cover chocolate-flavored cupcakes with Chocolate Fudge Frosting (see page 22), brightly-colored candies, and candy-covered chocolate drops.

Flying Kite

serves 20
decoration time 45 minutes

double quantity Butter Frosting (see page 21)

blue paste food coloring

9 inch deep round Large Madeira Cake
  (see page 13)

10 inch thick round cake board or plate

4 oz white ready-to-use icing

sifted confectioners' sugar, for dusting

3 oz deep blue ready-to-use icing

3 oz deep pink ready-to-use icing

small piece red ready-to-use icing or 1 tube
  red writing icing

Tip

Instead of a kite, draw an airplane on a piece of waxed paper, then cut off the wings. Roll out different colors for the body and wings and press on the cake, perhaps with a birthday banner tied to the back of the plane.

1 Color the butter frosting pale blue with the coloring. Trim the top of the cake level, if needed. Cut the cake horizontally in half and sandwich back together with some of the butter frosting. Put the cake onto the cake board or plate and spread the remaining butter frosting over the top and side, smoothing it with the back of a spatula.

2 Knead and roll out the white icing on a surface lightly dusted with confectioners' sugar. Cut out cloud shapes with a knife. Press over the top and side of the cake. Wrap the trimmings.

3 Cut a kite template from a piece of waxed paper or nonstick parchment paper about 4 inches along the top 2 edges and 5¼ inches along the lower 2 edges. Fold vertically in half to form 2 larger triangles and horizontally across the points to form 2 smaller triangles. Cut along the fold lines to separate the triangles.

4 Knead and roll out the deep blue icing and, using the kite template, cut out one smaller triangle from one side of the kite and one larger from the opposite side. Repeat with the deep pink icing. Press the triangles onto the cake top so that the kite tip overlaps the edge of the cake slightly. (If the kite tip begins to droop, prop it up with a rolled ball of foil and remove just before serving the cake.)

5 Shape most of the remaining blue icing into a long string and drape under the kite and over the edge of the cake. Cut out tiny triangles of pink icing and arrange in pairs for bows along the blue string.

6 Shape the reserved white icing into 2 oval eyes and press onto the kite, adding eyeballs shaped from the remaining blue icing. Shape the red icing into a mouth and press onto the kite, or pipe on a mouth with writing icing, if preferred.

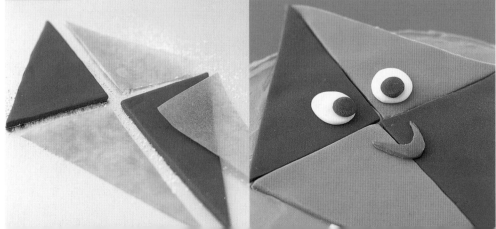

Tick-tack-toe

serves 9
decoration time 20 minutes, plus drying

5 oz red ready-to-use icing

sifted confectioners' sugar, for dusting

5 oz yellow ready-to-use icing

9 Cupcakes (see page 16) or bought cupcakes

single quantity Butter Frosting (see page 21)

12 inch square plate or thin cake board

7 wide strawberry-flavored gummy strips

1 Make a cross template by cutting a rectangle 2½ x 2 inches from paper or cardboard, then cut out a small triangle from the center of each long side and a larger triangle from each of the short sides.

2 Knead the red icing on a surface lightly dusted with confectioners' sugar until slightly softened. Roll out and cut around the template to make 5 crosses. Put onto a baking sheet lined with nonstick parchment paper lightly dusted with confectioners' sugar.

3 Knead and roll out the yellow icing and cut out 4 rounds with a 2 inch plain cutter. Stamp out a small circle from the center of each round using the end of a large cream piping tip or an upturned icing piping tip. Add to the baking sheet and leave to dry for at least 1 hour.

4 Spread the butter frosting over the center of the cupcakes and top with the dried icing shapes. Arrange on the plate or cake board with a grid made from the gummy strips, cut into appropriate lengths and overlapped as shown.

Tip
This idea could easily be adapted to make a crossword with stamped-out letters on a larger gummy-strip grid.

Magician's hat

serves 16
decoration time 1 hour

1 Trim the tops of the chocolate cakes level, if needed, then sandwich them together with some of the butter frosting. Spread a little of the remaining butter frosting over the side, filling in any gaps where the cakes join. Put onto the icing-covered cake board or plate.

2 Knead the black icing on a surface lightly dusted with confectioners' sugar until slightly softened. Roll out and cut a strip 22 x 6 inches or long and tall enough to go around the side of the cake stack. Carefully lift the icing and press onto the cake stack side. Trim off the excess, wrap and reserve.

3 Spread the uncovered cake board with a little butter frosting. Knead and roll out the gray icing and use to cover the top of the board. Roll out the reserved black icing into a strip 29 x 1½ inches and press onto the edge of the board for the hat rim, trimming off the excess. Stick the cake board onto the cake stack top with some butter frosting.

4 For the rabbit, cover the muffin with butter frosting and stick in place on the cake top with butter frosting. Cut a thin diagonal slice off each jelly roll and position on the cake for ears and paws, securing the ears with toothpicks for extra support, if necessary. Spread these with butter frosting.

5 Knead and roll out the pink icing, cut out ear and paw pads and press in place. Form a U-shaped mouth and press in place.

6 Add dolly mixture eyes and nose, pressing licorice bootlace whiskers under the nose. Stick rainbow pearl eyeballs to the eyes with a little butter frosting. Knead and roll out the white icing, cut out large and small stars and stick to the hat with the remaining butter frosting. Leave the icing to harden for a few hours before serving.

2 x 7 inch deep round chocolate-flavored Small Madeira Cakes (see page 12)

double quantity Butter Frosting (see page 21)

9 inch thin round cake board, covered with 12 oz mauve ready-to-use icing, or colored plate

1¼ lb black ready-to-use icing

sifted confectioners' sugar, for dusting

4 oz gray ready-to-use icing

9 inch thin round cake board

1 muffin (see page 17) or bought muffin, paper cup removed

4 bought mini chocolate, jelly, or vanilla jelly rolls

2 oz pink ready-to-use icing

1 round dolly mixture candy, halved

1 pink square dolly mixture candy

small piece black licorice bootlace, snipped into short lengths

2 pink rainbow pearls

3 oz white ready-to-use icing

Tip

Short of time? Then use three 6 inch store-bought chocolate layer cakes and a bought muffin and roll out black icing to fit the height and circumference of the cake stack.

Bunch of balloons

serves 8
decoration time 45 minutes

7 inch deep round Small Madeira Cake
  (see page 12)

single quantity Butter Frosting (see page 21)

8 inch thin round cake board or plate

13 oz orange ready-to-use icing

sifted confectioners' sugar, for dusting

1 oz red ready-to-use icing

1 oz deep blue ready-to-use icing

1 oz yellow ready-to-use icing

3 oz white ready-to-use icing

selection of different-colored narrow ribbons

1 Trim the top of the cake, if needed, then cut the cake horizontally in half and sandwich back together with some of the butter frosting. Put onto the cake board or plate. Reserve 2 teaspoons of the butter frosting and spread the remainder thinly over the top and side.

2 Knead the orange icing on a surface lightly dusted with confectioners' sugar until slightly softened. Roll out and use to cover the cake, smoothing in place with your fingertips dusted with confectioners' sugar. Trim off the excess, wrap and reserve.

3 Knead and roll out the red icing, cut out 2 balloon shapes and arrange on the cake top, with a piece of ribbon, about 6 inches long, tucked under each balloon. Repeat with the blue and yellow, then make one balloon with the white icing. Tie the balloon ribbons together with another ribbon, then trim the ends diagonally with scissors.

4 Shape the remaining white icing into a rope about 23 inches long. Repeat with the reserved orange icing, then twist the ropes together and press onto the base of the cake board, sticking in place with the reserved butter frosting.

Tip

Vary the colors of the balloons and cake to suit your child's favorite colors. You might also like to pipe on your child's name, piping a letter onto each balloon.

Candy-guzzling monster

serves 20
decoration time 50 minutes, plus drying

6 cup pudding basin Medium Madeira Cake
(see page 13)

7 inch deep round Small Madeira Cake
(see page 12)

one-and-a-half quantity Butter Frosting
(see page 21)

10 inch thick round silver cake board or plate

1½ lb white ready-to-use icing

sifted confectioners' sugar, for dusting

green paste food coloring

4 oz pale pink ready-to-use icing

4 oz purple ready-to-use icing

½ oz white ready-to-use icing

selection of candies and lollipops

Tip

To make a spooky Halloween version,
cover the cake in white icing and
add ghoulish black lips, eyeballs,
and eyebrows.

1 Level the basin cake top, if needed. Cut each cake horizontally in half and sandwich back together with butter frosting. Spread the top of the round cake with butter frosting, then transfer to the cake board or plate, positioning the cake slightly off-center close to the side of the cake board. Press the basin cake, trimmed top downward, on top.

2 Reserve 2 teaspoons of the butter frosting and spread the rest over the cake top and sides.

3 Knead the white icing on a surface lightly dusted with confectioners' sugar until slightly softened. Knead in a little green coloring until partially mixed and faintly marbled. Roll out into a 14 inch round. Lift on the rolling pin and drape over the cake so that it falls in folds, easing it down to the board with your fingertips, if necessary. Leave space between the front folds for the mouth.

4 Knead and roll out the pink icing thickly. Cut out 2 feet and tuck under the front of the green icing. Roll out the icing a little thinner and cut out an oval-shaped mouth 4 x 3 inches. Stick in place with a little water. Reserve trimmings for hands.

5 Knead and roll out one-third of the purple icing into a rope 5 inches long for the top lip, pinch together in 2 places, then stick onto the mouth with a little of the reserved butter frosting. Cut out an oval 5 x 3 inches from the remaining purple icing, dot the lower underside edges with butter frosting and stick onto the mouth to create a pouch.

6 Shape the purple icing trimmings into 2 arched eyebrows and 2 eyeballs. Shape the white icing into 2 eyes. Stick the features in place with water or butter frosting. Cut out hands from the reserved pink icing and stick to the front of the cake. Leave to dry for at least 30 minutes, then add candies to the mouth.

Older kids

Grand master

serves 20
decoration time 1 hour

8 inch deep square Large Madeira Cake
   (see page 13)

one-and-a-half quantity Butter Frosting
   (see page 21)

9 inch thin square cake board or plate

2 lb white ready-to-use icing

sifted confectioners' sugar, for dusting

4 oz dark blue ready-to-use icing

4 oz black ready-to-use icing

49 inches x 1 inch wide blue and white
   checked ribbon

Tip
As the chess pieces are relatively time-consuming to make, don't attempt to make a full set, but give the impression that a game is halfway through, with some of the pieces already taken.

1 Level the top of the cake, if needed. Cut the cake horizontally in half and sandwich back together with some of the butter frosting. Put onto the cake board or plate and spread the remaining butter frosting thinly over the top and sides.

2 Cut off 4 oz of the white icing, wrap and reserve. Knead the remainder on a surface lightly dusted with confectioners' sugar until slightly softened. Roll out and use to cover the top and sides of the cake, smoothing in place with your fingertips dusted with confectioners' sugar. Trim off the excess and add to the reserved white icing.

3 Knead and roll out the blue icing thinly to 4 x 8 inches. Cut vertically into eight 1 inch wide strips, then cut horizontally into 4 equal-size strips to make 32 squares. Arrange these on top of the cake in a checkerboard pattern with 4 in each row.

4 Make stylized chess pieces from the reserved white icing and the black icing based on different-size triangles of icing, adding tiny flattened balls of icing and rounded balls of different sizes for the pawns, bishop, king, and queen. Make a diagonal cut in the top of the bishop. Add different-shaped crowns to the king and queen and tiny castellated strips to the rook or castle. For the knight, add an oval head and cut a small strip with one side cut into a thin fringe for the mane. Add ears and stand on a small plinth.

5 Arrange the chess pieces on the cake to look as if a game is in progress, with a few pieces beside the cake board. Tie the ribbon around the side of the cake.

Rock fan

serves 12
decoration time 1 hour

1 Put the roasting pan cake, base uppermost, onto a large cutting board with the jelly roll pushed up against one of the short edges. Trim the large cake to resemble a guitar body (see picture opposite). Cut a guitar head from the cake trimmings.

2 Cut the guitar shape horizontally in half and sandwich back together with some of the butter frosting. Transfer to the cake board or tray, leaving space for the guitar "neck." Spread the top and sides thinly with more butter frosting and spread the rest over the head.

3 Knead the coffee-colored icing, roll out and use to cover the top of the guitar. Trim off the excess. Knead and roll out three-quarters of the dark brown icing and cut two strips each 9 x 2 inches. Press around the sides of the guitar, fitting the edges together at the top and bottom. Roll out and cover the head with the remainder. Add the jelly roll neck and the shaped head to the cake board or tray.

4 Knead and roll out the white icing. Cut out a rectangle 7 x 5 inches, then shape as in the picture. Press onto the guitar body. Cut 3 small string rests and 3 volume control knobs from the trimmings and press on. Cut a piece for the top of the head. Shape small balls of icing for string tighteners. Stick in place.

5 Roll out thin ropes of white icing and stick onto the jelly roll at intervals, adding flattened balls of icing in between with piped white icing. Pipe dots of icing over the string rests and add 6 silver balls to each.

6 Tie lengths of silver cord around the string tighteners and secure on the guitar with balls of icing. Snip off the excess and cover with a thick rectangular strip of white icing. Knead, roll out and cut black musical icing notes to decorate the board or tray.

12 x 9 x 2 inch roasting pan chocolate-flavored Medium Madeira Cake (see page 13)

11 inch chocolate-flavored Jelly Roll (see page 18) or 11 inch bought chocolate jelly roll

single quantity chocolate-flavored Butter Frosting (see page 21)

25 x 10 inch thin silver cake board or larger colored tray

12 oz coffee-colored ready-to-use icing

sifted confectioners' sugar, for dusting

12 oz dark brown ready-to-use icing

8 oz white ready-to-use icing

2 tablespoons Royal Icing (see page 25)

18 edible silver balls

13 feet fine silver cord

4 oz black ready-to-use icing

Tips

• The cake or cutting board required is such an unusual size that you may prefer to serve the cake on a large plastic tray instead and cover it with foil or colored foil wrapping paper.

• If you find that the cord for the guitar strings keeps unraveling, secure it around a halved toothpick, then cover this with icing, but make sure to remove it before cutting the cake.

soccer star

serves 10
decoration time 1 hour

2 x 4 cup pudding basin Medium Madeira
  Cakes (see page 13)

single quantity Butter Frosting (see page 21)

1 lb white ready-to-use icing

sifted confectioners' sugar, for dusting

9 inch thin cake board or round plate

4 oz black ready-to-use icing

4 oz blue ready-to-use icing (or color of your
  child's favorite team)

1 tube colored writing icing (optional)

Tips

- Roll out extra icing for the hexagons as
  necessary, keeping the remainder well
  wrapped to prevent it from drying out
  and making shaping difficult.
- The top of a spice jar makes an ideal
  circle template for the first stage of
  making the hexagon template.
- If using a cake board, you may like to
  cover it with green butter frosting or
  green-colored shredded coconut to
  resemble grass.

1 Level the basin cake tops, if necessary, and sandwich
together with some of the butter frosting to form a ball shape.
Reserve 1 tablespoon of the remaining butter frosting and
spread the remainder thinly over the outside of the cake.

2 Knead and roll out two-thirds of the white icing thinly. Use to
cover the cake, smoothing with your fingertips dusted with
confectioners' sugar. Trim off the excess, wrap and reserve.
Transfer the cake to the cake board or plate.

3 Create a hexagon template by cutting a 1½ inch round from
waxed paper. Fold the round in half, then fold the half into 3.
Cut a straight line between the ends of the fold lines, then
open out.

4 Knead and roll out a little of the black icing and cut out a
black hexagon. Press onto the cake top. Roll out a little of
the reserved white trimmings and cut out white hexagons,
arrange these around the black one and press or nudge the
shapes so that they fit exactly. Add a row of black hexagons,
then more white hexagons, sticking in place down the sides
of the ball with dots of the reserved butter frosting. As you
cover more of the cake, you may need to trim down the
hexagon shapes slightly to fit. Reserve a little white icing.

5 Knead and roll out the blue icing and cut out 3 rounds
of decreasing size with fluted cookie cutters, the largest
3 inches. Frill the edges by rolling a toothpick back and forth
over them. Press one on top of the other for the rosette. Add
a small round of the reserved white icing to the center. Cut
strips of the blue icing for the rosette tails. Arrange the rosette
by the side of the ball. Pipe your child's name or age onto the
center of the rosette, if desired.

speedy skater

serves 6
decoration time 45 minutes

4 chocolate-covered marshmallow teacakes

11 inch chocolate-flavored Jelly Roll (see page 18) or 11 inch bought chocolate jelly roll

10 inch thin square cake board, covered with 8 oz white or mauve ready-to-use icing, or mauve plate

2 tablespoons apricot jelly

single quantity Chocolate Fudge Frosting (see page 22)

4 oz yellow ready-to-use icing

sifted confectioners' sugar, for dusting

3 oz black ready-to-use icing

8 oz gray ready-to-use icing

Tips

- If you are planning to give some skates as a birthday present, then adapt the colors on the cake to match them.
- If you are putting the cake on an icing-covered board, you may find it easier to spread the jelly roll with fudge frosting before you move it to the cake board.
- For a smooth finish to the chocolate fudge frosting, use a small spatula dipped into boiling water when smoothing it.

1 Put the teacakes onto a cutting board and position the jelly roll just above so that the left-hand side aligns with the first teacake. Cut the jelly roll at an angle on the right-hand side, just behind the last teacake, for the boot heel. Put the trimming at right angles to the first piece to form the boot leg.

2 Shape the boot toe and put the trimming at the top of the boot leg to add extra height to the skate. Transfer all of the cakes to the cake board or plate. Spread the cut edges of the jelly roll with jelly.

3 Spread the fudge frosting over the top and sides of the jelly roll and smooth with a knife.

4 Knead the yellow icing on a surface lightly dusted with confectioners' sugar until slightly softened. Roll out and cut a strip 7 x 4 inches. Press onto the inside top of the boot leg for a lining tongue. Knead and roll out the black icing, cut a strip and press next to the yellow for the boot lining.

5 Knead and roll out two thirds of the gray icing and cut out a curved shape for the boot leg reinforcement. Drape over the boot leg and smooth in place. Cut a strip 5 x ¾ inch, mark with knife cuts, then press onto the boot leg for an adjustable strap. Make a small black clip with gray detail.

6 Roll out the remaining gray icing, cut a strip 8 x 2 inches and shape to make a wheel guard. Press halfway over the wheels and halfway over the boot base.

7 Cut 2 more strips for boot straps from the gray trimmings, press in place and add clips as in Step 5. Roll out the remaining black icing thinly, cut thin strips and squares and press onto the boot for molding detail. Roll small balls of yellow and gray, flatten and stick to the wheels and leg reinforcement with water for rivets.

Crashed skier

serves 8
decoration time 50 minutes, plus drying

2 oz gray ready-to-use icing

sifted confectioners' sugar, for dusting

3 oz black ready-to-use icing

toothpicks

2 oz red ready-to-use icing

½ oz pale pink ready-to-use icing

5 cup pudding basin Small Madeira Cake
(see page 12)

double quantity Butter Frosting (see page 21)

8 inch thin square cake board or plate

4 tablespoons shredded coconut

little black paste food coloring

Tips

- Remove the body and toothpicks before slicing the cake.
- If you are very short of time, use a washed child's action doll, cut the cake vertically in half and sandwich back together with the doll in the middle, or if using a broken doll, leave the cake whole. Put the clothes back on the doll once the cake has been iced.

1 Roll out the gray icing thickly and cut 2 skis 5 x ½ inch. Round one end of each ski and curl up slightly. Shape 2 thin ropes 4 inches long for poles, taper one end of each, then wrap a thin rope around a little way from the tapered end. Leave to harden on a baking sheet lined with nonstick parchment paper for 3 hours, or overnight.

2 Roll out the black icing thickly and cut 2 trouser legs 3 x ½ inch. Stick a toothpick into one end of each so that it extends about 1 inch. Stick gray ski boots to the other end with water. Leave to partially dry with the skis. Reserve the trimmings.

3 For the skier's arms and trunk, shape most of the red icing into a semicircle with a 2½ inch long base. Cut 2 cuts up from the base ½ inch in from either side but not all the way through and shape into outstretched arms. Shape the pink icing into a head with a small nose, adding a tiny skewer hole for the mouth. Add a black hat with red icing detail and attach to the shoulders with a toothpick. Shape a black scarf and gloves and add to the skier. Add 2 more toothpicks to the waist. Leave to dry.

4 Level the cake top, if needed. Cut horizontally in half and sandwich back together with a little butter frosting. Put the cake, trimmed top downward, onto the cake board or plate.

5 Reserve 1 tablespoon of the butter frosting and spread the remainder over the top and side of the cake, and a little over the board or plate.

6 Press the body into the top of the cake and the legs halfway down. Spread a little butter frosting over the trousers and body. Sprinkle the cake and skier with coconut. Attach skis to ski boots and poles to gloves. Paint on eyes with black coloring.

Chocolate extravaganza

serves 20
decoration time 30 minutes, plus drying

8 inch deep square chocolate-flavored Large
  Madeira Cake (see page 13)

single quantity Glossy Chocolate Butter
  Frosting (see page 22)

10 inch thick square cake board or plate

5½ oz bag white chocolate-covered malt balls

5½ oz bag milk chocolate-covered malt balls

1 Level the top of the cake, if needed. Cut the cake horizontally
in half and sandwich back together with a little of the frosting.

2 Put the cake on a wire rack set over a cookie sheet and pour
the remaining frosting onto the cake top. Gently spread over
the top and down the sides with a small spatula, scooping
up the frosting from the cookie sheet to fill in any gaps at the
base of the cake.

3 Carefully transfer the cake to the cake board or plate.
Arrange alternate-colored malt balls in diagonal rows over
the top of the cake, with a single row around the base of the
cake. Allow to set in a cool place for at least 30 minutes
before serving.

Tip
Vary the candies on top of the cake
according to your child's preference or
make the cake multicolored by adding
a variety of candies in different colors.

Hearts and flowers

serves 14–16
decoration time 30 minutes

1. Put the cake onto a cutting board and level the top, if needed. Make a waxed paper heart template by drawing around the cake board and cutting out the heart. Trim a little off all the way around the template edge until it fits the cake top. Cut the cake around the heart template.

2. Cut the cake horizontally in half and sandwich back together with some of the butter frosting. Transfer to the cake board. Spread the remaining butter frosting over the top and side of the cake.

3. Lightly knead the pale pink icing on a surface lightly dusted with confectioners' sugar until slightly softened. Roll out until a little larger than the cake. Lift on a rolling pin and drape over the cake, then smooth in place with your fingertips dusted with confectioners' sugar. Trim off the excess.

4. Re-knead the trimmings and roll out. Cut out flower and heart shapes of different sizes using plunger cutters, pressing them out onto a piece of foam sponge so that they curl (see page 32), then transfer to a baking sheet lined with nonstick parchment paper dusted with a little confectioners' sugar. Make dark pink or red and white flowers and hearts in the same way from the remaining ready-to-use icing.

5. Arrange the flowers and hearts over the cake top and stick in place with tiny dots of piping icing or piped royal icing. Add dots of icing to the center of some of the larger flowers and add candles. Tie the ribbon around the side of the cake and decorate the cake board with extra flowers and hearts.

9 inch deep round Large Madeira Cake (see page 13)

9½ inch thin heart-shaped cake board

one-and-a-half quantity Butter Frosting (see page 21)

1¼ lb pale pink ready-to-use icing

sifted confectioners' sugar, for dusting

3 oz deep pink or red ready-to-use icing

3 oz white ready-to-use icing

1 tube white piping icing or 2 tablespoons Royal Icing (see page 25)

pale pink candles

36 inches x 1 inch wide pink ribbon

Tip

For a St. Valentine's Day version, use a chocolate-flavored cake and cover it with a single quantity of Glossy Chocolate Butter Frosting (see page 22) and add red and pink hearts of varying size.

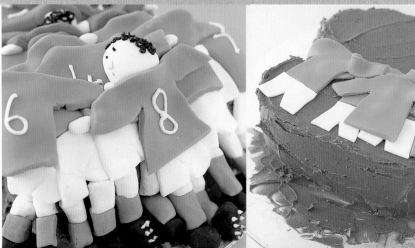

Rugby scrum

serves 14–16
decoration time 1¼ hours

1 Level the top of the cake, if needed. Trim off and round the corners to make an hour-glass shape, then slope the opposite sides of the cake slightly for the players to lean against.

2 Cut the cake horizontally in half and sandwich back together with butter frosting. Put the cake onto the cake board or plate. Spread butter frosting thinly over the top and sides and roughly on the board or plate to resemble a muddy pitch.

3 Knead the green (or favorite team's color) icing on a surface lightly dusted with confectioners' sugar until slightly softened. Divide into 10 pieces. Reserve 2 pieces for socks and roll each of the remaining pieces into a 2½ inch square. Make a small cut on either side of each square in from the bottom corner and almost to the top of the square, then shape into arms and a body. Arrange one row of 3 shirts facing the center of the cake, with arms stretched over the next player's shoulders. Knead and roll out the white icing and add a row of rectangular white shorts with a small slit in the base of each. Add a second row of 4 shirts and shorts a little back from the first, with the shirts curving over the edge of the cake. Add the eighth man to the center of the side of the cake. Repeat for the team on the other side of the scrum.

4 Knead the pink icing and shape a head for each player on the edge of the scrum and one or two extra heads with button noses and small holes for mouths. Shape hands for the players.

5 Shape short pink sausage shapes for thighs and same-sized pieces from the teams' colored icing reserved in Step 3 for socks. Add black oval pieces for boots. Shape a rugby ball from the remaining black icing and trim with white icing.

6 Pipe on black hair and facial features. Pipe white numbers onto the shirt backs and studs on some boots.

8 inch deep square chocolate-flavored Large Madeira Cake (see page 13)

one-and-a-half quantity chocolate-flavored Butter Frosting (see page 21)

13 inch thin round cake board or plate

12 oz green ready-to-use icing (or favorite team's color)

sifted confectioners' sugar, for dusting

12 oz red ready-to-use icing (or opponent team's color)

8 oz white ready-to-use icing

8 oz pink ready-to-use icing

5 oz black ready-to-use icing

1 tablespoon Royal Icing (see page 25), colored black, or 1 tube black writing icing

2 tablespoons white Royal Icing (see page 25) or 1 tube white writing icing

Tip

Modify the shirts, socks, and numbers to adapt this cake for American football and create ready-to-use icing helmets and shoulder pads for the players. Choose colors to match your favorite teams.

Funky boots

serves 10
decoration time 1 hour, plus drying

2 x 11 inch chocolate-flavored Jelly Rolls (see page 18) or 2 x 11 inch bought chocolate jelly rolls

3 tablespoons raspberry jelly

4–6 long wooden satay sticks

1 lb mauve ready-to-use icing

sifted confectioners' sugar, for dusting

7 inch square cake board or plate

4 oz pale pink ready-to-use icing

7 oz deep pink ready-to-use icing

1 Cut each jelly roll in half. Put two jelly roll halves a little apart on a cutting board for the boot feet. Stand a second half of jelly roll on top of one at one end for the boot leg and secure with jelly and satay sticks. Repeat to make a second boot leg. Shape the boot feet by trimming away a little of the cake.

2 Spread the cakes thinly with the remaining jelly. Cut the mauve icing in half, wrap one half and reserve. Knead the remaining half on a surface lightly dusted with confectioners' sugar until slightly softened. Roll out thinly and drape over one of the boots so that any joins will fall on the inside face of the boot. Smooth in place with your fingertips dusted with confectioners' sugar. Trim off the excess. Fill any gaps with trimmings. Cover the second boot in the same way. Carefully transfer to the cake board or plate.

3 Knead and roll out the pale pink icing. Cut out two 2½ inch rounds with a plain cookie cutter and press onto the top of the boot legs. Reserve the trimmings.

4 Knead and roll out the deep pink icing. Cut long strips ½ inch wide. Press one around the top of each boot and a second around the base of each boot, sticking in place with a little water, and trim off the excess.

5 Cut heart shapes from re-rolled icing trimmings using 3 different-size small cutters, then cut smaller shapes from the 2 larger ones. Stick in place with water. Leave for at least 1 hour for the icing to harden.

Tips

• If the boots seem a little wobbly, stand a tall sauce bottle or bag of flour behind each boot leg before leaving to dry. The boots are best iced the day before they are needed.

• Make sure you remove the satay sticks before serving the cake to guests.

Pretty purse

serves 14–16
decoration time 50 minutes

8 inch deep square Large Madeira Cake
   (see page 13)

one-and-a-half quantity Butter Frosting
   (see page 21)

14 x 10 inch rectangular cake board or
   large plate

1½ lb pale pink ready-to-use icing

sifted confectioners' sugar, for dusting

5 oz white ready-to-use icing

8 oz pale green ready-to-use icing

6 pink sugar flowers

Tip

For an adult version, use a favorite purse
as a guide and copy colors, clasp, and
handle detail.

1 Put the cake onto a cutting board and level the top, if needed. Cut a thin curved slice from the top 2 opposite sides of the cake to about one-third down the length of the cake. To do so, turn the first piece of trimmed cake over and use it as a template to cut the second side. Slope the top edge of the purse down toward the narrow side so that the edge where the flap will go is shallower.

2 Cut the cake horizontally in half and sandwich back together with two-thirds of the butter frosting. Put onto the cake board or plate. Reserve 2 teaspoons of the butter frosting and spread the remainder thinly over the top and sides of the cake.

3 Knead the pink icing on a surface lightly dusted with confectioners' sugar until slightly softened. Roll out thinly and use to cover the cake, smoothing with your fingertips dusted with confectioners' sugar. Trim off the excess, wrap and reserve.

4 Knead the white icing, roll out thickly and cut out the top flap of the purse. Press in place, smoothing with your fingertips. Reserve the trimmings.

5 Knead and roll out the pale green icing. Cut long strips ½ inch wide and stick as stripes onto the lower part of the bag with water, extending up to the flap and leaving space in between so the pink icing can be seen. Trim off the excess.

6 Cut a rectangle of pink icing 1½ x ½ inch and press onto the flap for a clasp. Cut a smaller green rectangle and add at right angles to the pink. Cut a white strip for a buckle. Stick flowers onto the flap with the reserved butter frosting.

7 Roll the remaining pink, white, and green icing into small balls and arrange alternate colors as a strap on the cake board, joining up to the purse top.

Chocolate bliss

serves 6
decoration time 45 minutes, plus drying

Shallow Cake (see page 17)

single quantity vanilla-flavored Butter Frosting
(see page 21)

10 inch round cake board, covered with 8 oz
deep pink ready-to-use icing, or plate

4 cup pudding basin Medium Madeira Cake,
made with half the 4-egg mixture
(see page 13)

1¼ lb turquoise-blue ready-to-use icing

sifted confectioners' sugar, for dusting

toothpicks

1½ oz milk or dark chocolate

1–2 teaspoons milk

few large marshmallows

3½ oz bag candy-covered chocolate drops

2 tablespoons Royal Icing (see page 25) or
1 tube writing icing

Tips
- Make sure you remove the toothpicks
  before serving the cake to guests.
- Colored spots, hearts, or flowers could
  be cut from colored ready-to-use icing as
  an alternative to the candy spots on the
  cup and saucer.

1 Spread the top and sides of the shallow cake thinly with
butter frosting and put on a cutting board. Level the basin
cake top, if needed, then place, trimmed top downward,
onto a cutting board. Cut horizontally in half and sandwich
back together with some of the butter frosting. Spread a
little more of the butter frosting thinly over the outside of the
basin cake.

2 Knead the turquoise-blue icing on a surface lightly dusted
with confectioners' sugar until slightly softened. Cut off 5 oz
and wrap and reserve the remainder. Roll out the measured
icing and use to cover the shallow cake, smoothing the
surface with your fingertips dusted with confectioners' sugar.
Trim off the excess. Transfer to the cake board or plate.

3 Roll out the remaining blue icing and drape over the basin
cake. Smooth over the surface, then carefully turn up the
other way to resemble a cup. Trim off the excess and smooth
the top edge. Put onto the shallow cake.

4 Re-knead the trimmings, roll into a thick rope 5 x ½ inch and
shape into a cup handle. Press onto the cup side and secure
with toothpicks. Prop up with pieces of crumpled foil.

5 Put the chocolate in a heatproof bowl and melt over a
saucepan half-filled with gently simmering water. Stir into the
remaining butter frosting, mixing in enough milk to make a
smooth glossy icing. Spread over the top of the cup and add
the marshmallows to the center.

6 Stick the colored chocolate drops over the cup and saucer
with piped dots of royal or writing icing. Leave to harden for
at least 1 hour. Remove the foil from under the cup handle
before serving.

white chocolate treats

serves 8
decoration time 45 minutes, plus chilling

1 Trim the top of the cake level then, using a 2½ inch plain cookie cutter or upturned tumbler as a template, cut out 8 smaller rounds of cake from the large cake using a small serrated knife. Cut each cake horizontally in half.

2 Add a spoonful of the white chocolate cream to 8 cake halves, then top with the remaining cake halves. Spread some white chocolate cream thickly over the top of each cake and then thinly around the sides.

3 Put the white chocolate in a heatproof bowl set over a saucepan half-filled with just-boiled water. Set aside for 5 minutes or so, off the heat, until the chocolate has melted. Cut 8 strips of nonstick parchment paper 8 x 3½ inches. Stir the chocolate, then spread over one strip right up to one long edge and then make a wavy swirled edge a little way down from the opposite long edge. With the wavy edge uppermost, press the strip of paper so that the chocolate touches the cream-spread edge of the cake and stands a little above the top. Smooth in place and repeat until all the cakes have been wrapped in the same way. Chill for 2 hours or until set.

4 Carefully peel the paper away from the chocolate, top the cakes with foil-wrapped candy and decorate the sides of the cakes with ribbon. Transfer to a plate or cake board. Chill in the refrigerator until ready to serve.

9 inch deep round Large Madeira Cake (see page 13)

single quantity White Chocolate Cream (see page 24)

8 oz white chocolate, broken into pieces

12 oz foil-wrapped candy

selection of thick and thin jewel-colored ribbons in 3 colors, such as purple, pale pink, and cerise pink

large round or square plate or cake board

Tips

- A dark chocolate version could be created in the same way, with small strawberries added to the tops of the cakes instead of the candy.
- The cake trimmings may be used for a trifle or could be eaten as a cook's perk!

Flowers and butterflies

serves 8
decoration time 1 hour, plus chilling/drying

2 oz white chocolate, broken into pieces

2 oz dark chocolate

4 oz pale pink ready-to-use icing

sifted confectioners' sugar, for dusting

7 inch deep round chocolate-flavored Small Madeira Cake (see page 12)

single quantity Double Chocolate Ganache (see page 23)

9 inch pale pink cake board or plate

Tip

If the butterflies seem a little soft when you take them out of the refrigerator, freeze them for 10 minutes. You may find it helpful to prop up the wings with some of the tiny pink flowers.

1 Put the white chocolate in a heatproof bowl set over a saucepan half-filled with just-boiled water. Set aside for 5 minutes or so, off the heat, until the chocolate has melted. Stir, then spoon into a nonstick parchment paper pastry bag and snip off the end (see page 31). Pipe pairs of butterfly wings, in the shape of a capital "B" with its mirrored reflection for the other wing, onto a cookie sheet lined with nonstick parchment paper. Fill in the centers with squiggly piped lines and pipe separate bodies, if desired.

2 Melt the dark chocolate in a separate bowl and use to pipe butterflies as before. Chill the decorations in the refrigerator for 45 minutes or until firm.

3 Meanwhile, knead the pale pink icing on a surface lightly dusted with confectioners' sugar until slightly softened. Roll out and stamp out flower shapes with 4 different-size cookie cutters ranging from 1¼ to 3 inches and some tiny flowers with plunger cutters. Curl the petals by pressing into sections of a muffin pan lined with crumpled nonstick parchment paper (see page 32). Leave to dry for 30 minutes.

4 Cut the cake horizontally in half and sandwich back together with some of the ganache. Transfer to the plate or cake board. Reserve 1 tablespoon of the ganache and spread the remainder over the top and side of the cake, smoothing with a small spatula.

5 Arrange the flowers over the top of the cake, with a few around the base of the cake. Carefully lift the butterfly wings off the paper and arrange in the flowers with dots of piped ganache, then add the bodies to the butterflies, if using. Add pale pink flower candles in between the flower and butterfly icing decorations, if desired.

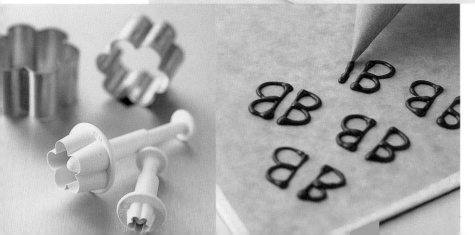

Bowled over

serves 12
decoration time 45 minutes

12 x 9 x 2 inch roasting pan Medium Madeira
   Cake (see page 13)

one-and-a-half quantity Butter Frosting
   (see page 21)

13 x 10 inch rectangular cake board, covered
   with 12 oz royal blue ready-to-use icing,
   or plate

1½ lb white ready-to-use icing

sifted confectioners' sugar, for dusting

7 oz black ready-to-use icing

3 oz orange ready-to-use icing

2 oz turquoise ready-to-use icing

1 Put the roasting pan cake on a cutting board so that the short edges are facing you. Cut a little off the top left- and right-hand sides to resemble the necks of 3 bowling pins, standing close together. Shape the bottom short edge into 3 curves for the pin bases.

2 Cut the trimmed cake horizontally in half and sandwich back together with some butter frosting. Put onto the cake board or plate and spread the top and sides thinly with the butter frosting.

3 Cut off 8 oz of the white icing, wrap and reserve. Knead the remaining icing on a surface lightly dusted with confectioners' sugar until slightly softened. Roll out and use to cover the cake, smoothing in place with your fingertips dusted with confectioners' sugar. Trim off the excess.

4 Re-knead one-third of the icing trimmings, roll out and cut into a tall pin shape, the height of the cake and about one-third the width. Press onto the left-hand side of the cake top.

5 Knead and roll out the remaining white icing and cut out 2 more pin shapes. Add one to the right-hand side of the cake, then press the third in the center.

6 Knead and roll out the black icing. Cut out thin strips and use to edge the sides of the pin markings and decorate the top. Stick in place with a little water. Reserve the trimmings.

7 Knead and roll out the orange icing. Cut out small rectangles and 3 narrow strips. Use to decorate the pins. Knead and roll out the turquoise icing and cut into a 4 inch circle. Position on top of the pins for the ball. Roll out the reserved black trimmings, cut out a number for the age of the birthday child, then press onto the ball.

Tip
If your child is a member of a bowling club, then match the markings on the pins with those at the bowling alley.

Riding champ

serves 8–10
decoration time 1 hour

1 Level the cake top, if necessary. Turn the cake over, trimmed top downward, cut into 3 horizontal layers and sandwich together with butter frosting. Reserve 2 teaspoons of butter frosting and spread the remainder thinly over the top and side of the cake. Spread the reserved butter frosting over half the cake board.

2 Knead the black icing on a surface lightly dusted with confectioners' sugar until slightly softened. Cut off 2 oz and wrap. Roll out the remainder until it covers half the cake board. Drape over the butter-frosted end of the cake board for the hat peak and smooth with your fingertips dusted with confectioners' sugar. Trim off the excess. Re-knead the trimmings and roll out. Cut out 2 ribbons for the back of the hat and 2 small buttons. Transfer to a sheet of nonstick parchment paper.

3 Put the cake onto the cake board so that it almost touches the un-frosted end and slightly covers the black "hat peak" end.

4 Draw a triangular template for the colored silks on nonstick parchment paper with a base 4½ inches long and a height of 6 inches. Cut out.

5 Knead the pale pink icing, roll out and use the template to cut out 3 triangular shapes. Press lightly onto the cake, leaving spaces in between. Cut out 3 deep pink triangles and press into the gaps, readjusting the position of the triangles slightly as necessary, trimming away the excess or pressing the edges together so that the cake is neatly covered. Smooth with your fingertips dusted with confectioners' sugar.

6 Put the cake board onto a plate and place the black ribbons at the back. Roll out the reserved black icing and cut a strip 21 x ¾ inches. Stick around the base of the hat with a little water. Add a black button to back and top.

6 cup pudding basin Medium Madeira Cake (see page 13)

single quantity Butter Frosting (see page 21)

9 x 7 inch thin oval cake board or plate

8 oz black ready-to-use icing

sifted confectioners' sugar, for dusting

8 oz pale pink ready-to-use icing

8 oz deep pink ready-to-use icing

Tip
You may like to add a ribbon or icing rosette to finish off the cake, with the age of your child or a birthday message piped or written onto the center. See page 74 for details of how to make a rosette from ready-to-use icing.

Ice cream dream

serves 12
decoration time 50 minutes

12 x 9 x 2 inch roasting pan chocolate-
   flavored Medium Madeira Cake
   (see page 13)

double quantity vanilla-flavored Butter Frosting
   (see page 21)

14 x 10 inch rectangular cake board, covered
   with 12 oz lilac ready-to-use icing, or plate

1 lb pale yellow ready-to-use icing

4 chocolate-flavored Muffins (see page 17)
   or large bought muffins

pink or red paste food coloring

green paste food coloring

brown paste food coloring

1 To make the cone, cut the roasting pan cake into a triangle 7 x 9 inches on a cutting board. The trimmings are not needed (see Tip).

2 Cut the cone horizontally in half and sandwich back together with some of the butter frosting. Spread the top and sides thinly with butter frosting. Transfer the cone to the cake board or plate.

3 Knead the yellow ready-to-use icing on a surface lightly dusted with confectioners' sugar until slightly softened. Roll out two thirds, drape over the cone to completely cover and smooth in place. Trim off the excess and knead with the remaining icing. Roll out and use to cover the left half of the cone. Smooth in place and trim off the excess. Mark the icing with criss-cross lines to resemble a wafer.

4 Trim a vertical slice off 2 of the muffins, then set against the cone, with a third muffin above them. Trim a slice off the base of the remaining muffin and set aside.

5 Divide the butter frosting into four portions, leaving one plain. Color the second pink, the third pale green, and the remaining portion light brown. Spread each color over a different muffin and arrange as ice cream scoops, with the trimmed edges fitted next to the cone.

Tip

To make use of the cake trimmings, split and sandwich them together with extra butter frosting, spreading some on top too. Cut into small shapes and decorate with candy. Alternatively, use the sponge cake as the base for a trifle or tiramisu.

Gifts galore

serves 28
decoration time 1¼ hours

1 Level the cake tops, if needed. Cut each cake horizontally in half and sandwich back together with butter frosting. Put the square cake onto the cake board and spread the top and sides thinly with a little butter frosting. Reserve 1 tablespoon of the butter frosting and spread the remainder over the other 2 cakes. Put these cakes aside.

2 Cut off one-quarter of the burgundy icing, wrap and reserve. Knead the remaining icing on a surface lightly dusted with confectioners' sugar until softened. Roll out and use to cover the square cake, smoothing in place with your fingertips dusted with confectioners' sugar. Trim off the excess and reserve.

3 Cut off one-third of the white icing, wrap and reserve. Use the remainder to cover the larger round cake. Trim off the excess and reserve. Put on top of the square cake.

4 Cut off one-quarter of the blue icing, wrap and reserve. Use the remainder to cover the small round cake. Trim off the excess and reserve. Put on top of the other cakes.

5 Roll out the reserved blue icing and cut 4 strips 3½ x 1 inch. Stick to the sides of the base cake with butter frosting, to resemble ribbons. Trim the tops of the strips where they touch the round cake. Reserve the trimmings.

6 Make burgundy ribbon strips for the center cake and white strips for the top cake in the same way. Cut an extra strip of white and form into 2 loops for a bow, adding 2 smaller strips for the ribbon ends.

7 Roll out the remaining blue icing trimmings and cut tiny rounds with the upturned end of a piping tip. Stick over the center cake with a little water. Cover the top of the cake board with a strip of white icing (see page 29). Stick the ribbon onto the side of the cake board with sticky tape.

8 inch deep square Large Madeira Cake (see page 13)

1 x Small Madeira Cake mixture (see page 12) split between 1 x 6 inch deep round pan and 1 x 3½ inch small baked bean can (see Tips), baked

double quantity Butter Frosting (see page 21)

10 inch thick square cake board

1½ lb burgundy ready-to-use icing

sifted confectioners' sugar, for dusting

1 lb white ready-to-use icing

8 oz pale blue ready-to-use icing

36 inches x ½ inch narrow white ribbon

double-sided sticky tape

Tips
- Use a 7 oz baked bean can for the tiny cake.
- Remove the top and bottom of the baked bean can before use, wash well and peel away the label. Stand it on a baking sheet and line with nonstick or waxed paper as if lining the base and sides of a larger pan (see page 11).

Animal magic

My little kitten

serves 10
decoration time 30 minutes

2 small layer cakes (see page 15), each filled
with 2 tablespoons jelly, or 2 bought filled
vanilla or chocolate layer cakes

12 x 10 inch oval cake board or large plate

double quantity Butter Frosting (see page 21)

red and yellow or orange food coloring

2 jumbo green candy-coated chocolate beans

2 standard brown candy-coated chocolate
beans

6 chocolate sticks

4 oz orange ready-to-use icing

sifted confectioners' sugar, for dusting

1 Put one cake onto the cake board or plate for the body then
prop the second up against it for the cat's head.

2 Spoon one third of the butter frosting into a separate bowl
and color it orange.

3 Spread the head and body with the remaining uncolored
butter frosting, then spoon on some orange butter frosting to
create the effect of ginger markings, easing it into stripes and
swirls with the tip of a small knife.

4 Press the green candy eyes in position, then stick on brown
candy eyeballs with a little butter frosting. Break a little off
the end of the chocolate sticks and press into the cake for
whiskers. Knead the orange ready-to-use icing on a surface
dusted with a little confectioners' sugar. Shape a small
ball into a nose shape, then use more icing to create two
triangular ears, four round paws, and a thin rope for the
mouth. Mark the paws with a knife and add to the cake.

Tip
If the cake is very crumbly, spread it with
a little jelly before topping with the butter
frosting so that the crumbs are stuck in place.

Puppy love

serves 10
decoration time 1 hour, plus drying

5 cup and 3 cup pudding basin Medium
   Madeira Cakes (see page 13)

10 inch thin round cake board or plate

double quantity vanilla-flavored Butter Frosting
   (see page 21)

toothpicks

4 bought mini jelly rolls

8oz bar white chocolate

½ oz white ready-to-use icing

sifted confectioners' sugar, for dusting

1½ oz black ready-to-use icing

½ oz red ready-to-use icing

4 oz pale yellow ready-to-use icing

Tip
Make sure you remove the toothpicks
before serving the cake to guests.

1 Level the basin cake tops, if necessary. Put the larger one, trimmed top downward, onto the cake board or plate for the dog's body. Spread the outside with a little of the butter frosting. Put the smaller cake on top, trimmed top downward, slightly off center for the head, and secure with butter frosting and toothpicks.

2 Scoop out eye sockets in the top cake with a teaspoon and shape a small muzzle. Stick 2 jelly roll front legs at the front of the cake with a little butter frosting and the remaining 2 toward the back for back legs.

3 Reserve 3 teaspoons of the butter frosting and spread the remainder all over the cake to cover completely.

4 Run a swivel-bladed vegetable peeler over the smooth underside of the chocolate bar to create curls (see page 32). Stick the curls all over the dog with a dull knife.

5 Roll small balls of white icing for the eyes, flatten into ovals and press in place. Add tiny balls of black icing for eyeballs and stick in place with dots of butter frosting. Shape the remaining black icing into a round nose and stick onto the muzzle. Mark with the end of a toothpick. Shape the red icing into a curved tongue and add to the face.

6 Roll out two-thirds of the yellow icing thickly and cut out floppy ears. Stick in place with a little of the reserved butter frosting, propping them up with pieces of crumpled foil or nonstick parchment paper. Roll a ball of yellow icing, cut in half and make 3 small cuts in each half. Add to the front legs for paws. Shape 2 larger back paws from short sausage shapes and add cuts as before. Shape the remaining icing into a tail and press in place. Leave for at least 30 minutes for the ears to harden, then remove the foil or paper before serving.

Cute teddy

serves 8
decoration time 45 minutes, plus drying

4 cup pudding basin chocolate-flavored
  Medium Madeira Cake, made with half the
  4-egg mixture (see page 13)

10 x 8 inch oval cake board or plate

toothpicks

1 large chocolate Muffin (see page 17), or a
  large bought muffin, paper cup removed

2 bought mini chocolate jelly rolls

2 bought ladyfingers

single quantity Chocolate Fudge Frosting (see
  page 22)

4 oz pale blue ready-to-use icing

sifted confectioners' sugar, for dusting

2 foil-wrapped chocolate coins, unwrapped, or
  2 jumbo chocolate buttons

½ oz white ready-to-use icing

2 blue mini candy-covered chocolate drops

1 brown candy-covered chocolate drop

pink paste food coloring

2 sugar flowers

20 inch fine ribbon (optional)

Tip
Make sure you remove the ribbon and
toothpicks before serving the cake to
birthday guests.

1 Level the basin cake top, if necessary. Put it, trimmed top downward, onto the cake board or plate. Press 3 toothpicks into the domed top of the cake, then press the muffin onto the sticks so that the rounded top is facing forward for the bear's head. Add the mini jelly rolls for the legs and ladyfingers for the arms, attaching to the cake with more toothpicks.

2 Reserve 2 teaspoons of the fudge frosting. Spread the remainder over the cake and rough up with the back of the knife so that it resembles fur. Leave for a few minutes to harden slightly.

3 Knead the blue icing on a surface lightly dusted with confectioners' sugar until slightly softened. Roll out and cut out a waistcoat shape. Press onto the bear, adjusting the shape of the waistcoat, if necessary, with scissors.

4 Re-knead the trimmings. Roll small balls for the paws, flatten, then press onto the ends of the arms and legs. Add tiny flattened balls to the feet for claws.

5 To make the ears, press a small flattened ball of blue icing on to each chocolate coin or button, then press into the top of the head. Shape tiny flattened ovals of white icing for eyes and add mini candy-covered chocolate drops for eyeballs, sticking in place with dots of the reserved fudge frosting. Add the brown candy-covered chocolate drop for the nose. Color the remaining white icing pink, roll out and cut out a mouth shape. Press onto the bear's face. Add the sugar flowers for buttons, sticking in place with dots of fudge frosting. Complete with a ribbon around the neck, if desired.

Mini duck ponds

makes 12
decoration time 30 minutes

12 Cupcakes (see page 16), or bought
    cupcakes

single quantity Glacé Icing (see page 24)

blue paste food coloring

3 tablespoons shredded coconut

green paste food coloring

10 oz yellow ready-to-use icing

sifted confectioners' sugar, for dusting

1 oz orange ready-to-use icing

2 tablespoons Royal Icing (see page 25),
    colored green, or 1 tube green writing icing

10 inch round cake board or plate

1 Level the cake tops, if necessary. Color the glacé icing blue
with the coloring, then spoon onto the cake tops and smooth
with the back of the spoon.

2 Put the coconut in a small bowl with a little of the green
coloring and mix with a spoon until pale green. Sprinkle
around the edges of the blue icing "ponds."

3 Knead the yellow icing on a surface lightly dusted with
confectioners' sugar until slightly softened. Tear off small
pieces and make 12 oval-shaped duck bodies 1 inch long
and 12 small oval heads ¾ inch long. Press the heads onto
the bodies and stick in place with a little water, if necessary.

4 Re-knead the trimmings, roll out and cut out six 2 inch rounds
with a fluted cookie cutter. Cut each round into quarters, then
stick a pair of quarters on each duck as wings, with the
fluted edge as the wing tips, using a little water.

5 Knead and roll out the orange icing. Shape tiny triangular
beaks and stick onto the ducks with a little water. Sit the
ducks on the mini ponds and use royal or writing icing to
pipe on green eyes. Transfer to the cake board or plate.

Tip

As an alternative, Easter-themed, design,
you could make smaller wings and
transform the ducks into chickens, then sit
them on nests of crumbled chocolate flake
with mini chocolate eggs in the center.

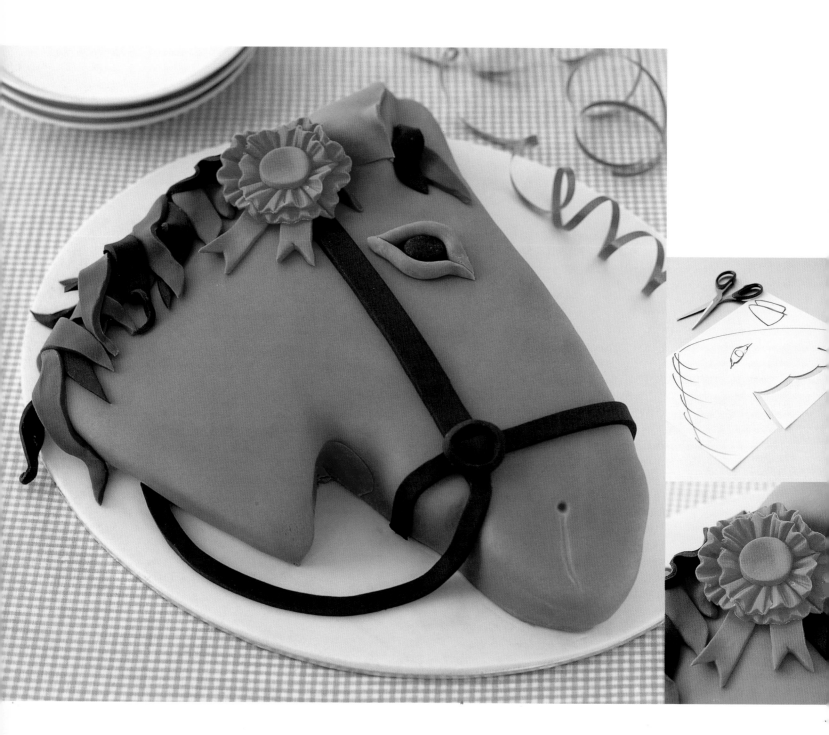

My first pony

serves 8–10
decoration time 45 minutes

1 Draw a horse's head on a piece of paper the same size as the cake. Cut it out and use as a template to cut the shape from the cake. Cut two triangular ears from the trimmings.

2 Cut the cake horizontally in half and sandwich back together with some of the butter frosting. Spread the remaining butter frosting thinly over the top and sides of the cake, adding the ears and covering them with butter frosting. Transfer to the cake board or plate.

3 Knead the brown icing on a surface lightly dusted with confectioners' sugar until slightly softened. Roll out the icing and use to cover the cake. Smooth in place with your fingertips dusted with confectioners' sugar. Trim off the excess. Re-knead and wrap the trimmings. Mark a mouth with the handle of a small brush.

4 Knead and roll out the black icing. Cut strips for bridle and reins and place on the cake, sticking in position with a little water. Cut a circle of icing with an upturned piping tip then cut out a smaller circle with another piping tip. Position where the reins meet the bridle at the mouth.

5 Roll out a little of the brown trimmings, and cut out 2 brown ears and an eye socket. Press on to the cake, adding a black eyeball. Knead extra brown coloring into the remaining brown icing to darken. Re-roll the dark brown and black trimmings and cut petal shapes for the mane. Stick on to the neck with water. Add a red rosette (see page 74), if desired. Pipe your child's name or age onto the rosette, if desired.

12 x 9 x 2 inch roasting pan chocolate-flavored Medium Madeira Cake (see page 13)

one-and-a-half quantity Butter Frosting (see page 21)

15 x 13 inch oval cake board, covered with 1 lb pale green ready-to-use icing, or a plate

1 lb brown ready-to-use icing

sifted confectioners' sugar, for dusting

5 oz black ready-to-use icing

brown paste food coloring

4 oz red ready-to-use icing (optional)

Tip

For a child who is regularly taking riding lessons, adapt the coloring to suit their favorite pony at the stables.

Scary shark

serves 12
decoration time 1 hour

12 x 9 x 2 inch roasting pan Medium Madeira
    Cake (see page 13)

11 x 9 inch thin oval cake board

one-and-a-half quantity Butter Frosting
    (see page 21), colored red

1 lb black ready-to-use icing

sifted confectioners' sugar, for dusting

4 oz white ready-to-use icing

2 yellow and black licorice candies

black paper

14 x 12 inch cake board or plate

Tip
Use black paste food coloring for a really
dark color or buy ready-colored black
icing from specialty cake-decorating stores.

1 Put the cake onto a cutting board so the top is uppermost
and the short sides are facing you. Measure 5 inches up
from the bottom left-hand corner, repeat on the other side and
7½ inches up in the center then cut between the marks in an
arched line. Set aside for the shark's head. Cut a 4 inch deep
semicircle from the remaining cake, using the uncut edge as
the base, for the jaw. Discard the trimmings.

2 Put the jaw onto the cake board with the curved edge almost
touching one end. Graduate the straight edge of the back of
the jaw so the other cake section will sit comfortably, then place
the shark's head on top, half on the jaw, half off, to make the
mouth. Fill in the gaps underneath the top cake with trimmings.

3 Spread the mouth area of the cakes thickly with butter frosting,
then spread the rest thinly over the top and sides of the cake.

4 Knead and roll out one-third of the black icing to a long strip
and trim to 15 x 2 inches. Carefully lift and press around the
jaw base and a little over the head base, smoothing in place
with your fingertips. Roll out the remaining icing, curve one
edge and press the curved edge up to the curved edge on
top of the shark's head. Drape over the sides, down to the
back of the cake board, and smooth in place. Trim off the
excess icing and reserve.

5 Cut triangles for teeth from the thinly rolled white icing. Press
the top teeth in place first, then the bottom teeth. Add 2
licorice candy eyeballs. Shape 2 black eyelids and press
over the eyeballs. Cut 3 fins 7 inches long and a tail 17
inches long from black paper. Fold along the base of one fin
and stand on the cake top. Put the other 2 fins and tail on the
large cake board or plate, place the shark cake on top then
curl the end of the tail so that it stands up.

Timid tortoise

serves 8
decoration time 1 hour

1 Level the cake top, if necessary. Put, trimmed top downward, on to a cutting board, cut horizontally in half and sandwich back together with some of the butter frosting. Spread a little butter frosting thinly all over the top and side of the cake then put it onto the cake board or plate.

2 Make a hexagon paper template by cutting a circle of paper 1¾ inches in diameter. (The top of a spice jar is an ideal size for this.) Fold in half then into three to make six segments. Cut a straight line from each tip of the fold to the other then open out.

3 Cut off one-quarter of the yellow icing, wrap and reserve. Knead the remaining yellow icing on a surface lightly dusted with confectioners' sugar until slightly softened. Roll out thinly. Repeat with the pink and blue icing.

4 Cut out several hexagons. Put one yellow hexagon in the center of the cake then arrange alternate-colored shapes in 3 rings around the tortoise's shell, rolling and cutting the icing trimmings until the tortoise is completely covered.

5 Knead the remaining pink icing and shape four small legs and a head. Position against the cake. Knead and roll out the reserved yellow icing, shape into a long rope, then flatten with a rolling pin and trim to 25 inches long by ½ inch wide. Press around the base of the tortoise's shell. Shape the tortoise's eyes and eyelids from blue and pink icing and stick onto the cake with water. Make a mouth with a toothpick.

6 Decorate the cake board with sugar flowers, cut with different-size plunger cutters (see page 32), if desired.

8 inch mixing bowl Small Madeira Cake (see page 12)

one-and-a-half quantity Butter Frosting (see page 21)

11 inch thin round cake board, covered with 12 oz pale green icing, or plate

12 oz pale yellow ready-to-use icing

sifted confectioners' sugar, for dusting

12 oz pale pink ready-to-use icing

5 oz pale blue ready-to-use icing

few sugar flowers (optional)

Tip
You may find it easier to roll out small pieces of colored icing with a child's rolling pin, making just enough hexagons for one ring at a time so that they don't dry out as you stick them on.

Fearless lion

serves 14–16
decoration time 30 minutes

9 inch deep round Large Madeira Cake
   (see page 13)

1 bought mini jelly roll

10 inch thin round cake board or plate

double quantity Butter Frosting (see page 21)

yellow paste food coloring

red paste food coloring

black paste food coloring

8 oz bar dark or milk chocolate

5 oz white ready-to-use icing

2 yellow and black licorice candies

Tips

- The butter frosting could alternatively be colored and flavored with about 4 teaspoons cocoa powder dissolved in 1 tablespoon boiling water instead of using the food coloring, if preferred.
- If you are very short of time, use pieces of chocolate flake for the lion's mane and ready-colored ready-to-use icing.

1 Trim the top of the large round cake level, if needed. Put the cake onto a cutting board and lay the mini jelly roll on top in the center for the lion's nose. Make 2 inverted "V" cuts, each about 2 inches deep and 2 inches apart, beneath the nose to make the lion's jaw. Reserve the trimmings for the ears. Round the jaw with a small knife, then round the cheeks on either side.

2 Transfer the cake to the cake board or plate. Stick the ears in place with a little butter frosting.

3 Reserve 1 teaspoon of the butter frosting. Color the remainder orange using a little each of the yellow and red colorings, then spread all over the top and side of the cake.

4 Turn the chocolate bar over so that the smooth side is uppermost. Run a swivel-bladed vegetable peeler over the smooth side to make curls (see page 32). Press the chocolate curls around the top edge of the cake for the lion's mane using the flat edge of a dull knife.

5 Knead and roll 2 small balls of white icing, flatten and shape into thin ovals, then press onto the face for eyes. Add the candies for eyeballs, sticking them in place with a little of the reserved butter frosting.

6 Color two-thirds of the remaining white icing deep orange, shape into a curled tongue and press in place. Color the remaining icing black, shape into 2 flat rounds, then press on to the base of the nose. Add small indentations with the end of a toothpick. Store in a cool place until ready to serve.

Dancing dolphins

serves 10
decoration time 1 hour

Large round Quick-mix Layer Cake
(see page 14)

double quantity Butter Frosting (see page 21)

10 inch round cake board or plate

12 oz white ready-to-use icing

sifted confectioners' sugar, for dusting

ice blue paste food coloring

8 oz dark blue ready-to-use icing

36 inches x 1½ inch wide blue chiffon ribbon

1 Sandwich the cakes together with a little butter frosting, then spread butter frosting thinly around the side. Put onto the cake board or plate.

2 Knead the white icing on a surface lightly dusted with confectioners' sugar until slightly softened. Knead in a little blue coloring until a pale even blue, then mix in a little more coloring until marbled with blue streaks.

3 Shape the icing into a long rope, then flatten with a rolling pin and trim to a strip 26 x 4 inches. Press around the side of the cake, pressing the extra width over the top edge of the cake. Trim off any excess from the join.

4 Partially mix a little blue coloring into the remaining butter frosting until it becomes marbled. Reserve 1 tablespoon of the frosting, then swirl the remainder over the top of the cake to resemble the sea.

5 Knead the dark blue icing until softened slightly. Shape into 2 dolphins about 5 inches long by making a thick sausage shape and squeezing a nose at one end and a tapering tail at the other. Next, shape a dolphin head about 2½ inches long. Shape the remaining icing into small fins. Stick onto the dolphins with a little water or dots of butter frosting. Make eyes by pressing a toothpick into the icing.

6 Arrange the dolphins on the cake, propping them up on pieces of pale blue icing so they look as if they are jumping. Spread the reserved butter frosting around the icing support to resemble lapping waves. Tie the ribbon in a pretty bow around the cake.

Tip
Instead of dolphins, why not try modeling a boat with a fisherman or a sailor onboard out of ready-to-use icing?

Seasonal treats

Valentine cupcakes

makes 12
decoration time 30 minutes

single quantity Butter Frosting (see page 21)

pink paste food coloring

12 Cupcakes (see page 16) or bought
   cupcakes, with silver foil paper cups

7 oz red ready-to-use icing

sifted confectioners' sugar, for dusting

10 chocolate sticks

3 oz pale pink ready-to-use icing

large round or square plate

1 Color the butter icing pale pink with a little of the coloring. Level the tops of the cakes, if needed. Spread the tops of the cakes with an equal quantity of the butter frosting.

2 Knead the red icing on a surface lightly dusted with confectioners' sugar until slightly softened. Roll out and cut out twelve 2 inch hearts with a cookie cutter, re-kneading and rolling out the trimmings as necessary.

3 Press the heart shapes onto 10 of the cakes. Cut the remaining 2 hearts in half with a zigzag line to symbolize a broken heart. Separate the halves slightly, then press onto the 2 remaining cakes.

4 For Cupid's arrows, break each chocolate stick in half, press one half into the center of each unbroken heart and the other half as if coming out of the edge of the cake. Knead and roll out the pink ready-to-use icing, cut out triangular arrow tips and "V"-shaped feathers and stick onto the chocolate sticks with a little water or with tiny dots of butter frosting from the scrapings in the bowl. Arrange on the plate and sprinkle the plate with heart-shaped foil graffiti, if desired.

Tip
Instead of adding the Cupid's arrows, pipe on boys' and girls' names with tubes of colored writing icing.

Easter bunnies

makes 12
decoration time 30 minutes

12 Cupcakes (see page 16) or bought
    cupcakes

single quantity Butter Frosting (see page 21)

12 large white marshmallows

4 large pink marshmallows

12 mini white marshmallows

24 blue mini candy-covered chocolate drops

12 small square pink candies

2 tablespoons Royal Icing (see page 25),
    colored red, or 1 tube red fine
    writing icing

1 oz pale pink ready-to-use icing

sifted confectioners' sugar, for dusting

large round or square plate

1 Level the tops of the cakes, if needed. Spread the tops of the cakes with an equal amount of the butter frosting.

2 Cut the large white marshmallows in half. With the cut side uppermost, squeeze the corners to form into ear shapes. Press 2 onto each cake, cut side uppermost. Cut the pink marshmallows in half, then each half into slices. Press a slice on top of each ear.

3 Cut the mini white marshmallows in half and press the cut sides downward onto the rabbit faces for cheeks. Add blue candy-covered chocolate drops for eyes and square pink candies for noses. Pipe a mouth onto each rabbit with red royal or writing icing.

4 Knead the pale pink icing on a surface lightly dusted with confectioners' sugar until slightly softened. Roll out and cut tiny strips for whiskers. Press onto the rabbits. Arrange on a plate and store in a cool place until ready to serve.

Tip

To save time on a party day, the cakes may be made in advance, spread with the butter frosting and then frozen. Add the facial features once the cakes have been defrosted.

Ghostly ghoul

serves 10
decoration time 30 minutes

1 Put the cake onto a cutting board and cut into a long oval face shape. Curve the sides slightly to indicate hollow cheeks and a jaw. Cut the cake horizontally in half and sandwich back together with some of the butter frosting. Spread the remaining butter frosting thinly over the top and sides of the cake.

2 Cut off 7 oz of the white icing, wrap the remainder and reserve. Knead on a surface lightly dusted with confectioners' sugar until slightly softened. Add a little black coloring and knead until partially mixed and marbled. Roll out the icing thinly, drape over the cake board and smooth with your fingertips dusted with confectioners' sugar. Trim off the excess.

3 Lift the cake onto the board. Pull off small pieces of the reserved white icing and shape into sausage shapes. Press onto the cake for eyebrows, lips, nose, and frown lines. Roll out the remaining white icing and drape over the cake to cover completely, smoothing over the raised areas with your fingertips dusted with confectioners' sugar. Trim off the excess.

4 Color the trimmings black. Roll out a small ball of icing and cut a heart-shaped nose. Divide the remaining icing into thirds and shape each third into a small sausage. Flatten and shape into eyes and a mouth. Press onto the cake, sticking in place with a little water.

12 x 9 x 2 inch roasting pan Medium Madeira Cake (see page 13)

double quantity Butter Frosting (see page 21)

1¼ lb white ready-to-use icing

sifted confectioners' sugar, for dusting

black paste food coloring

12 x 10 inch oval cake board

Tip
You may find it easier to dust the cake board with a little confectioners' sugar and roll the marbled icing straight onto the board with a rolling pin.

spooky spiders

makes 12
decoration time 1 hour

12 Cupcakes (see page 16) or bought
    cupcakes, with silver foil paper cups

single quantity Butter Frosting (see page 21)

1 lb purple ready-to-use icing

sifted confectioners' sugar, for dusting

18 black licorice "wheels"

12 chocolate-covered marshmallow teacakes

24 pink candy-covered chocolate drops

24 mini blue candy-covered chocolate drops

1 tube black writing icing

large round or square plate

4 oz pink or dark blue ready-to-use icing

1 Level the tops of the cakes, if needed. Spread the top of each cake with a little butter frosting. Knead the purple icing on a surface lightly dusted with confectioners' sugar until slightly softened. Roll out and stamp out twelve 2½ inch rounds with a plain cookie cutter. Press one on top of each cake. Re-knead and roll out the trimmings. Stamp out twelve 1½ inch plain rounds and press one onto each cake for a head.

2 Add a little butter frosting to the center of each cake. Unroll the licorice and cut into 4 inch lengths. Add to each cake for legs. Cover the ends on each body with a teacake.

3 Stick 2 of the larger pink candy-covered chocolate drops on to each head for eyes with a little butter frosting. Add the mini blue candy-covered chocolate drops for eyeballs and pipe black vertical lines down the center with writing icing and tiny V-shaped nostrils.

4 Transfer the spiders to a plate and add small balls of pink or blue icing to the ends of the licorice legs for feet.

Tip

For children who do not like licorice, snip colored gummy strips, such as those used for the grid in the Tick-Tack-Toe cake on page 60, into legs instead.

Jack-o-lantern

serves 8
decoration time 30 minutes

8 inch mixing bowl Small Madeira Cake (see page 12)

double quantity Butter Frosting (see page 21)

yellow and red or orange paste food colorings

9 inch thin round cake board or large plate

2 oz black ready-to-use icing

sifted confectioners' sugar, for dusting

4 oz green ready-to-use icing

1 Color the butter frosting orange with a little each of the yellow and red or orange colorings. Cut the cake horizontally in half and sandwich back together with some of the butter frosting. Transfer the cake to the cake board or plate.

2 Spread a little of the butter frosting thinly all over the cake to stick the crumbs in place, then spread thickly with more of the butter frosting and smooth in downward lines with the back of a knife.

3 Knead the black icing on a surface lightly dusted with confectioners' sugar until slightly softened. Roll out and cut out a large smiling mouth. Cut out small squares or triangles for missing teeth. Press onto the cake. Cut out triangles for eyes and a nose and press in place on the cake.

4 Knead and roll out the green icing. Cut out leaves of different sizes, mark on veins with a small knife then arrange on the cake top, curling and folding them slightly. Re-knead and roll out the trimmings. Cut long thin strips and curl these in and around the leaves to resemble tendrils.

Tip
Add the coloring little by little; you will find that you need less paste coloring than when coloring ready-to-use icing.

Playful polar bears

serves 20
decoration time 1 hour, plus drying

9 inch deep round Large Madeira Cake
    (see page 13)

one-and-a-half quantity Butter Frosting
    (see page 21)

11 inch thin round cake board or plate

1½ lb pale blue ready-to-use icing

sifted confectioners' sugar, for dusting

single quantity Royal Icing (see page 25)

3 tablespoons shredded coconut

8 oz white ready-to-use icing

black writing icing or an edible black icing pen

Tip

This cake could also be made into a teddy's tea party by covering the cake in pale green ready-to-use icing, coloring the royal icing pink and spreading it into a smaller table-cloth shape. Add yellow bears and a dolls' house tea service with tiny plates and cups.

1 Trim the top of the cake level, if needed. Cut the cake horizontally in half and sandwich back together with butter frosting. Put it on the cake board or plate and spread the remaining butter frosting over the top and side of the cake.

2 Knead the blue icing on a surface lightly dusted with confectioners' sugar until slightly softened. Roll out and use to cover the top and side of the cake. Smooth in place with your fingertips dusted with confectioners' sugar. Trim off the excess.

3 Spoon the royal icing over the top of the cake and spread it so that it dribbles over the sides. Ease into icicle-like shapes with the point of a knife. Spread a little icing in patches on the board or plate and up the side of the cake. Sprinkle with the coconut, letting some fall onto the cake board or plate.

4 Knead the white ready-to-use icing until slightly softened. Shape 5 different-size ovals of icing for the polar bear bodies. Shape 5 round heads and make a small pinch in each for a muzzle. Press the heads onto the bodies. Arrange on the cake, sitting, lying or stretching up the side of the cake. For the standing bear, you may need to attach the body to the side of the cake with some royal icing scrapings from the bowl. Shape sausage-like arms and legs, making them slightly thicker where they join onto the body. To make the ears, roll tiny balls of icing, then flatten and press onto the heads, sticking in place with a little water. Roll any remaining trimmings into snowballs of various sizes.

5 Allow the bears to harden, then pipe or write on face details with black writing icing or an icing pen.

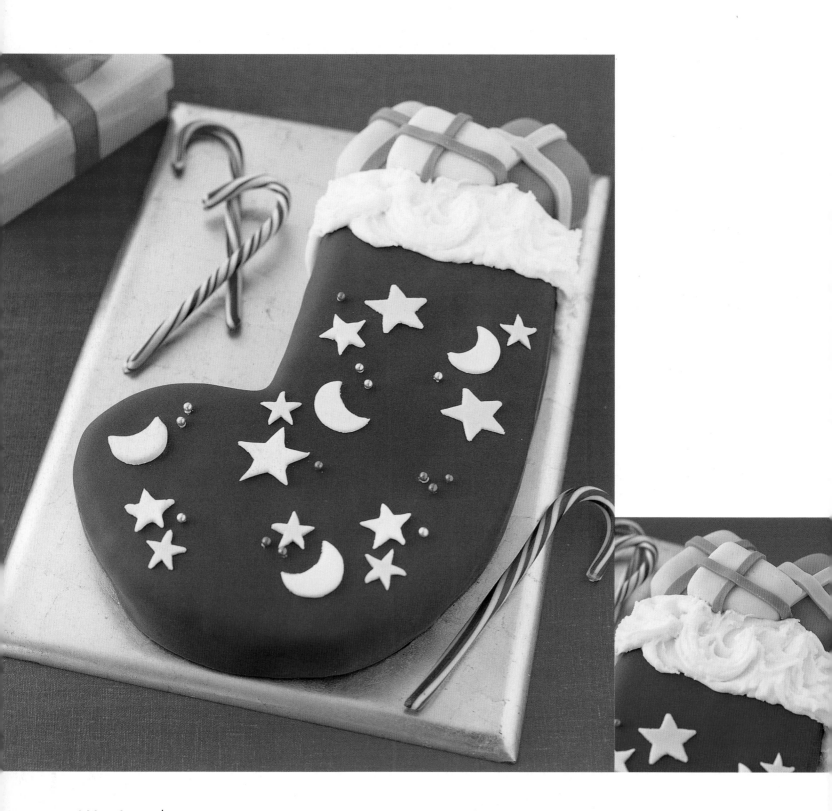

Christmas stocking

serves 10
decoration time 1 hour

1 Put the cake onto a cutting board and cut into a stocking shape about 4½ inches wide at the top of the leg. Cut 3 different-size gifts from the trimmings and set aside. Cut the cake horizontally in half and sandwich back together with some butter frosting. Spread a little butter frosting very thinly over the top and sides of the cake and over the gifts. Transfer the stocking cake to the cake board or plate.

2 Knead the deep blue icing on a surface lightly dusted with confectioners' sugar until slightly softened. Roll out and drape over the whole of the cake and smooth in place with your fingertips dusted with confectioners' sugar. Trim off the excess.

3 Spread most of the royal icing over the top of the stocking and down both sides, then rough it up so that it resembles fleecy lining. Spoon the remaining icing into a waxed paper pastry bag and snip off the end (see page 31).

4 Knead and roll out the white icing and cut out rounds using a small round cookie cutter, then cut partway into the rounds to make crescent moons. Cut star shapes with different-size cutters. Stick the shapes onto the stocking with piped dots of royal icing. Repeat with a little pale pink icing. Add extra dots of piped icing and stick on rainbow pearls or silver balls.

5 Knead and roll out the deep pink, pale blue, and remaining pale pink icings and cover one gift in each color. Cut ribbons from the trimmings and stick onto the gifts with royal icing. Position at the top of the stocking. Add the candy canes to the cake board or plate.

12 x 9 x 2 inch roasting pan Medium Madeira Cake (see page 13)

double quantity Butter Frosting (see page 21)

14 x 10 inch rectangular cake board or plate

12 oz deep blue ready-to-use icing

sifted confectioners' sugar, for dusting

half quantity Royal Icing (see page 25)

3 oz white ready-to-use icing

3 oz pale pink ready-to-use icing

few rainbow pearls or edible silver balls

2½ oz deep pink ready-to-use icing

2 oz pale blue ready-to-use icing

selection of candy canes

Tip
If using a cake board, you may like to cover it with pale pink ready-to-use icing before adding the cake.

Smiling snowman

serves 12
decoration time 1 hour

2 x 4 cup pudding basin Medium Madeira
    Cakes (see page 13)

single quantity vanilla-flavored Butter Frosting
    (see page 21)

2 tablespoons apricot jelly

6 inch thin round cake board or plate

1 Muffin (see page 17) or bought large muffin,
    paper cup removed

triple quantity Royal icing (see page 25)

½ oz black ready-to-use icing

sifted confectioners' sugar, for dusting

1 oz orange ready-to-use icing

2 oz red ready-to-use icing

1 oz yellow ready-to-use icing

Tip

The snowman can alternatively be
sandwiched together and covered with a
double quantity of vanilla or lemon butter
frosting (see page 21) instead of royal icing.

1 Level the basin cake tops, if necessary, and sandwich the
trimmed tops together with the butter frosting to make the
snowman's body. Spread jelly thinly all over the outside of
the cakes to stick the crumbs in place. Stand the cake upright
on the cake board or plate. Press the muffin onto the body so
that the domed part of the muffin forms the snowman's face.
Spread the muffin with the remaining jelly.

2 Spoon the royal icing over the cakes to cover completely,
spreading it as you go with a dull knife and pulling it into
peaks with the back of the knife. Be careful not to smear the
jelly into the icing.

3 Knead the black icing on a surface lightly dusted with
confectioners' sugar until slightly softened and shape black
eyes and "coal" buttons. Press onto the snowman. Knead the
orange icing and shape a tiny piece for the snowman's
"carrot" nose. Press onto the snowman's face.

4 Knead the red icing, shape a tiny rope mouth and add to
the face. Shape half the remaining red icing into a round
and press onto the snowman's head for a hat.

5 Knead the yellow icing and shape into a rope 7 inches long.
Repeat with the remaining orange and red icing. Twist the 3
colors together, then roll out to flatten. Trim to a 14 x 1 inch
strip. Make small cuts in either end for a fringe, then wrap
around the snowman as a scarf. Re-knead and roll out the
trimmings, fringe one side, then roll up and add to the top of
the hat for a bobble.

Index

Acknowledgments

Executive Editor Nicola Hill
Editor Leanne Bryan
Executive Art Editor Karen Sawyer
Designer Lisa Tai
Photographer Lis Parsons
Home Economist Sara Lewis
Props Stylist Rachel Jukes
Senior Production Controller Martin Croshaw
Picture Library Manager Jennifer Veall

PICTURE ACKNOWLEDGMENTS

Special Photography:
© Octopus Publishing Group Limited/Lis Parsons.

Other Photography:
© Octopus Publishing Group Limited/Gareth Sambidge 16 bottom